Can You Read Me?

of related interest

Support Groups for Older People Who Have Been Abused
Beyond Existing
Jacki Pritchard
ISBN 1 84310 102 5

Male Victims of Elder Abuse
Their Experiences and Needs
Jacki Pritchard
ISBN 1 85302 999 8

Becoming a Trainer in Adult Abuse Work
A Practical Guide
Jacki Pritchard
ISBN 1 85302 913 0

The Therapeutic Potential of Creative Writing
Writing Myself
Gillie Bolton
ISBN 1 85302 599 2

Creative Writing in Health and Social Care
Edited by Fiona Sampson
ISBN 1 84310 136 X

Creative Therapies with Traumatized Children
Anne Bannister
ISBN 1 84310 155 6

Narrative Approaches to Working with Adult Male
Survivors of Child Sexual Abuse
The Clients', the Counsellor's and the Researcher's Story
Kim Etherington
ISBN 1 85302 818 5

Writing My Way Through Cancer
Myra Schneider
ISBN 1 84310 113 0

Can You Read Me?

Creative Writing with Child and Adult Victims of Abuse

Edited by Jacki Pritchard and Eric Sainsbury

Jessica Kingsley Publishers
London and Philadelphia

First published in the United Kingdom in 2004
by Jessica Kingsley Publishers
116 Pentonville Road
London N1 9JB, England
and
400 Market Street, Suite 400
Philadelphia, PA 19106, USA

www.jkp.com

Copyright © Jacki Pritchard and Eric Sainsbury 2004

Library of Congress Cataloging in Publication Data

Pritchard, Jacki.
    Can you read me? : creative writing with child and adult victims of abuse / Jacki Pritchard and Eric Sainsbury.-- 1st American pbk. ed.
        p. cm.
    Includes bibliographical references and index.
    ISBN 1-84310-192-0 (pbk.)
    1. Creative writing--Therapeutic use. 2. Abused children--Rehabilitation. 3. Adult child abuse victims--Rehabilitation. 4. Self-actualization (Psychology) I. Sainsbury, Eric Edward. II. Title.
    RC489.W75P75 2004
    616.85'822306--dc22

                                                    2004000480

British Library Cataloguing in Publication Data

A CIP catalogue record for this book is available from the British Library

ISBN 1 84310 192 0

Printed and Bound in Great Britain by
Athenaeum Press, Gateshead, Tyne and Wear

This book would not have been possible without the original compositions of the following people and without their willingness to share their writings, thoughts and feelings with us. It was not always an easy experience for them, but they always met us with friendliness and trust. We shall remember them and our meetings with gratitude and great respect. This book is therefore dedicated to:

Open Door Children's Group (Girls)	Catherine, aged 10
	Emma, aged 12
	Francesca, aged 11
	Sinead, aged 14
Open Door Children's Group (Boys)	David, aged 10
	Liam, aged 10
	Ryan, aged 10
Open Door Writers' Group	Alex, aged 17
	Carla (age not known)
	Gemma, aged 18
Reach Out Project	Amanda, aged 20
	Jo, aged 19
	Steven, aged 23
	Thomas, aged 29
Individual contributors	Beccy, aged 26
	Indie Larma, aged 32
	Laura, aged 46
	Sue, aged 44
Beyond Existing	Beryl, aged 74
	Denise, aged 40
	Pat, aged 62
	Phyllis, aged 55
	Rita, aged 66
	Vera, aged 67

Our thanks and best wishes to you all.
JP and ES

Acknowledgements

We wish to acknowledge our indebtedness to Chris Hanvey, Director of Operations at Barnardos, and his colleague, Pam Hibbert, and especially to the Barnardos staff in the North:

Fiona Brown
Carol Butler
Edna Davis
Caroline Waitt
James Brooks

and their local colleagues. Their enthusiasm in their work has been inspirational and their support for this book, and to ourselves personally, has been patient and unstinting.

Similarly we wish to express our best thanks to everyone associated with Beyond Existing but in particular to Shaun Davidson and Janice Ward.

The Joseph Rowntree Foundation has supported Beyond Existing as part of its programme of research and innovative development projects, which it hopes will be of value to policy makers and practitioners. The facts presented and views expressed in this book are, however, those of the authors and not necessarily those of the Foundation.

Finally, a word of sincere appreciation to Jan Smith for her skills in typing and retyping substantial parts of the book, and for introducing Eric Sainsbury to various bits of electronic wizardry.

Contents

Glossary of Terms

Abuse   Abuse will include child abuse, domestic violence and adult abuse. Forms of abuse will include: physical, sexual, emotional/psychological, neglect, financial and discriminatory.

Author   In this book the word refers to anyone who has allowed us to publish their original work.

Carers   We are using this word very broadly to include field and residential social workers, people responsible for day care and group settings, foster parents, care workers in homes for those with special needs, aftercare hostels etc.

Leader   A person who leads a group or exercise.

Member   A person who attends a group.

Participant   A person who engages in an exercise.

Session   Meeting of group.

Victim   A person who has experienced abuse at some point in their life. The term is not used in a negative way. Nor does it imply personal incapacity.

Worker   Any person who is involved in working with a victim of abuse.

Writer   As for Author (above).

Symbols Used in this Book

The following symbols are used throughout this book for ease of recognition:

    Handouts

    Exercises

Work from Beyond Existing

A Note from the Editors

In discussion with the writers, we agreed to preserve the integrity of their work by not imposing an editorial polish. Some of the work may therefore appear to need editing. We ask the reader to remember the circumstances in which it was written and that, in poetry particularly, ambiguity is sometimes a true coinage.

JP and ES

CHAPTER 1

What It's All About

**...a chance to meet Sue, Amanda and Jo,
and to examine with them the value and limitations
of self-expression. Proceed with caution: things
aren't always what they seem**

This book presents the original compositions of several authors: some old, some young; some suffering with problems of health, disability or a sense of social exclusion. Some feel intensely isolated even when surrounded by family and friends. All in all, the authors are a heterogeneous collection of people.

They have, however, two things in common: their experiences of abuse and their use of original writing. The abuse has been of various kinds – physical, sexual, neglect, fear – but all arising from the degrading and dehumanising behaviour of other people, and all leading to an erosion of self-esteem and confidence. Yet, despite these problems, all the contributors to this book have, in some measure, 'risen above' their situations and their writing has been one of the means they used to achieve this. Each wrote their original composition to objectify – to some extent – the trauma of their experiences and to regain control over their feelings and, thus, their lives. They have found that what can be defined in language can be controlled in experience; that our language sets the boundaries of our understanding of experiences. This book therefore represents a bid to be understood; but it also sometimes demonstrates individual triumphs over serious adversity.

We need to recognise, however, that language has its limitations, both as a means of controlling one's feelings and as the means of setting conceptual boundaries around one's experiences. These limitations vary between individuals in their importance and intensity. Some people are verbally more sophisticated than others – though, in some situations, all of us find ourselves at a loss for words, however sophisticated we normally are. Sometimes, the limitations of our language indicate the presence of intense ambivalence: conflicting ideas carry equal weight and, in verbal terms, seem to invalidate each other. Sometimes, the sheer horror of a situation means the words tumble out without the imposition of logic.

The limits of language

The difficulty of finding the right words has been well expressed by one writer:

> ### Talking
> *By Sue*
> We have the tools for speech
> But seldom use them as we should.
> For when you talk you are no longer
> At peace with your own thoughts.
> Cease to dwell in your mind
> But go forth with acceptance
> Of that which is natural.
> There are those who talk
> Without knowing that they reveal the truth
> Which they do not understand.
> And there are those who know the truth within them
> But cannot say in words.

For Amanda, however, horror and ambivalence are of such intensity as to create a kind of verbal indigestion. Amanda has written about her father and what he did to her several years ago. She is left with an insoluble mixture of feelings:

Alone Yet Again

I TRY TO GO TO SLEEP AT NIGHT,
BUT I ALWAYS END UP HAVING A FRIGHT
I'm thinking of you all the time,
Oh how on earth could you.
You are very sick, really sick in the head.
You've put me through a lot of pain
When I was younger
And I'm getting the pain now
When I am older.
Memories don't just go away
I need someone to help it fade away.
The abuse you put me through
Has made me mad
I couldn't control the things you had
I was only a child, remember that?
You've made me angry
And so afraid
That I can really, really behave
Behave like an adult should be able to do
But I'm thinking always of you.
Oh just can't you see
I just want, want to be me.
My head's messed up with stuff from the past
Which all came to me as a blast.

Amanda expresses her fear that the past may be repeated; it is constantly reiterated when she goes to bed; her anger is intense; she feels confused about her potential for maturity. As she says, her head is all messed up. Past and present cannot easily be distinguished, and she sees no way of escape. For her, the limitations of self-expression are painfully evident and her poem reflects 'work in progress' rather than a sense – or even a hope – of achievement.

The purpose of the book

To some extent this book may be regarded as a training manual. It has two allied purposes: to sensitise the reader to what traumatic experiences *really* mean to the people who live through them; and to suggest some basic approaches and skills to carers who receive writings from the people they care for, and who wonder how to use them – both as a means of understanding and as a means of help. Much has already been written on the therapeutic benefits of creative writing, but very little on its use by the recipient. We hope that we can help those working in various therapeutic and care settings to recognise the value of creative writing, and more particularly to develop a fuller understanding of their own roles in empathising with others' feelings, in meeting others' emotional needs and in enhancing opportunities for resolving the problems of the past. We are concerned with how to create healing relationships, and how to enable an abused person to find hope and self-esteem in facing the future.

One matter needs to be cleared up at the start. We recognise that the processes involved in encouraging somebody to write constructively about their painful experiences, and in interpreting or reflecting back the essential meanings of what has been written, are highly skilled professional tasks. We recognise that a book of this kind cannot be a substitute for the kind of training that would be desirable. So we need to stress the limitations of what we are offering to the reader. Basically, our interest is in promoting sensitive and helpful responses to writings that have been spontaneously offered, either individually or – more probably – in the context of a writing group; several support agencies, particularly in the voluntary sector, now offer writing groups within their programmes of social activities. Formal training opportunities are rarely available for the people who organise these groups; this book is a modest compensation for this lack, and an expression of encouragement and fellow feeling.

Why do we sound so cautious? In our experience, it is all too easy to encourage people to write about experiences of abuse, pain and resentment. There is the popular belief that a trouble shared is a trouble halved – a remarkably persistent and misleading old saw. The real issue, which is seldom addressed, is how to ensure that personal disclosure is a positive experience which will be positively used. In coming to grips with this issue, we find that both common sense answers and the answers implicit in some theoretical formulations are often defective. Part of the answer lies in boundary-setting. Without some boundaries, people may feel pushed into making larger disclosures than they intend to make; and this in turn leads either to resentment of the person who encouraged them to go 'over the top', or to increasing dependency on the perceived kindness of the helper or therapist. Social work research gives useful examples of the dangers of excessively disclosing and exploring feelings: see, for example, Sainsbury, Nixon and Phillips (1982) and their reference to the work of Reid and Shyne (1969). Even more sinister is the risk that neither the author nor the helper will be able to control and constructively use the flow of material. The flow can sometimes be scary simply because it is out of control. The first aim in social care is not to do harm; encouraging excessive intense disclosures – irrespective of the good intentions of the helper – is a powerful source of harm.

Be ready to back off

Another area of risk and caution is that of naïve interpretation. Someone gives us a poem reflecting a painful episode. We respond glibly that we understand what he or she is saying. If simplistic, our 'understanding' is both an insult to the author and bogus as a means of helping: it reflects *our* need to be helpful, or – worse – our need to control or limit the processes of helping, rather than the author's need for help. Related to this is the response of the helper who eagerly 'fits' the writing (and the author) into theoretical constructs which may be wholly inappropriate. It is true that there is nothing more practical than a good theory; but defining a 'good' theory and recognising the limitations of *all* theories are areas of wisdom into which few venture, and we do not pretend to have ventured there ourselves.

The pitfalls of a naïve or false 'understanding' have been painfully indicated by Jo, when writing about an undoubtedly well-meaning social worker.

Fakers

They act like they care,
Oh they do care,
But only about themselves,
They'll be sorry, so so sorry.

They'll regret the day they met me.
The day they slagged me off.
I may be shy and scared,
But I WILL KILL THEM!

I CAN'T BELIEVE THEY LIE TO ME,
Everytime I see them.
But I don't care about that,
I don't need their friendship.

So it behoves us all to proceed with caution. And with a sense of humility.
Our co-authors have been willing to share their experiences and
thoughts with us; we recognise that our understanding is, at best, only
partial; and we are in the business of learning from them.

In our view, the aim of creative writing in social caring locations and
activities can best be expressed in moral rather than theoretical terms: it is
to respond in ways that the author feels are helpful; that lead to a sense of
self-esteem and personal control; that indicate that the author is understood and feels healed on his or her own terms and in his or her own
language. In moral terms, it is useful to remind ourselves of the limitations
of good advice (even when we give it with the best of intentions); and to
remind ourselves also that a subsidiary meaning of the Greek verb 'to
heal' (from which we derive the word 'therapy') is 'to honour'.

As Laura put it: 'Words have the power to harm, and the power to
heal.' And, as Rhodes has suggested (1986), we need to avoid
quasi-therapeutic situations where our language implies moral judge-
ments even though we intend to sound benign and value-free.

CHAPTER 2

Issues and Practicalities in Preparing the Book

Idea for the book

The idea to write this book came after setting up the organisation Beyond Existing which runs support groups for adults who have been abused (for more detail see Chapter 3). It was clear both in the pilot project and the ongoing work that creative writing was a medium through which some victims of abuse could voice their feelings and work towards and through a healing process. It also seemed probable that there are workers in various settings who, with training, could run similar support groups and thereby help a large number of adults who are not currently offered long-term support or who have to wait a considerable length of time for access to counselling or therapy. Hence came the original idea to write a book that could be used to help prepare workers to undertake such work, with special reference to the uses of creative writing. We were particularly influenced by the writings of Vera, a member of Beyond Existing. She has written extensively on her life, finding it easier to commit her feelings to paper than to express them in discussions, other than with one of the group leaders with whom she shares her writings. Much of her work is emotionally powerful and merits a wider audience; and when we thought about it, it seemed likely that others in similar situations might be helped to come to terms with their experiences in a similar way.

Inevitably, widening the age range of the project followed upon our learning that writing groups for young people existed in various parts of the country. We also guessed that some people, not members of groups, may be writing about their painful experiences as a 'do-it-yourself' form of therapy.

Starting the project: our sources

In addition to the Beyond Existing groups, whose members had already produced extensive journal writings and poetry, we sought contributions through advertising in magazines and newsletters within the voluntary sector inviting people to send their work to us. The proposed project was also discussed with people who worked with vulnerable adults in a variety of work settings so that anyone who wished would be given the opportunity to submit their work.

We knew that gaining access to children would quite properly be more difficult. Following discussions with managers and staff of two national organisations providing services for children, we were able to reach agreement about the scope and safeguards of our intentions, and were grateful for the opportunities and enthusiasm offered by Barnardos, who put us in touch with three writing projects.

These discussions highlighted some practical issues which, on reflection, indicate important professional and ethical concerns. One was the underlying danger of writing a book on so sensitive a subject: namely, that the complexities of therapeutic help might become oversimplified, and that we might be thought to encourage practices that were falling below adequate professional standards. This is a realistic fear, and is reflected in the caution we have expressed in Chapter 1.

A related issue was one concerning the skills of the staff who are, in formal terms, 'unqualified'. Our view on this matter is pragmatic: some 'unqualified' staff in our experience possess considerable understanding and interpersonal skills, and with the right support can help people to disclose the abuses they have suffered and can offer helpful ongoing support. Our aim is to help promote both thoughtfulness and confidence within the work, which many unqualified staff are already doing.

A further concern is whether and how the kind of therapeutic work described in this book can be linked to the complex framework of legal duties and responsibilities which underpin the provision of many welfare services. We recognise that much statutory work falls outside the scope of unqualified staff: notably child protection, where legal duties and public responsibilities are exclusively allocated to suitably qualified workers. We recognise also that qualified workers may not have the time for the kind of therapeutic work with which this book is concerned. Our association with Barnardos has provided examples of shared work between statutory and voluntary agencies, and of work combining the exercise of legal responsibilities with the provision of therapeutic help. It has also demonstrated successful partnerships between qualified and unqualified staff. In general terms, we believe that, within and between the service sectors, a similar sharing is possible which utilises the skills and availability of staff, irrespective of their formal qualifications. This is a matter of imaginative management and, of fundamental importance, of professionally competent supervision, which enables possibilities of teamwork between qualified and unqualified staff.

In a time when public welfare resources are fully stretched, there is a strong case for workers in all settings to pool their abilities in order to ensure the best and most comprehensive services to people who need them. Properly supervised partnerships between qualified and unqualified workers form part of this.

Finally, there needed to be discussions about the theoretical underpinning of our work. In the present book, our position – both ethical and in practice – is made as clear as possible. We acknowledge there are other approaches to the use of creative writing as a means of help. We were fortunate to find groups of workers whose approaches were compatible with our own.

Working with Barnardos

A draft proposal was discussed with senior and regional managers, and, with their agreement, with leaders of the creative writing groups. The objectives set out in the proposal were threefold:

- To prepare a book for social care workers interested in the use of creative or therapeutic writing among service-users.

- To demonstrate how this activity can be used to supplement and enhance more conventional modes of communicating feelings and needs; how it can promote understanding between writer and helper; and how it can help to put negative experiences into perspective, in the hope of neutralising their impact on present and future living.

- To offer service-users an opportunity of having their work published and, perhaps, to take pride in contributing to social care training.

Two projects were identified in the North of England which ran writing groups; we met the managers and the staff who run the groups for children and young people in the Open Door Project and for young adults in the Reach Out Project (for details about the projects see Chapter 3). We received a warm welcome from staff in both projects, who were enthusiastic about the idea of giving young people the opportunity to have their work published.

In the light of these discussions, certain procedures were agreed. First, an interview would be held with each potential contributor, either individually or in small groups according to the contributors' choice; each interview would be appropriately supervised by the attendance of a group leader or (in the case of young people) a parent. The interview would cover such matters as the origins of the writing, the feelings embodied in it, the intended audience (if there was one), the message it was hoped to convey, and the level of personal satisfaction experienced in the act of writing (both in the present and, possibly, in planning further writing). Second, it was agreed that edited versions of the published works and any additional comments would be sent in draft to the author for comment, correction and approval. Third, the authors' views would be sought in more general terms about the value of writing for others as well as for themselves.

We also discussed certain contingent ethical and psychological issues: for example, we needed to ensure that the children's sharing of their work with us would not exacerbate any residual emotional problems; the dangers and risks to which we have alluded in the last chapter would certainly be present, both in the interviews and the editing. Furthermore, publication of highly charged experiences could be damaging to the writers' continuing relationship with others whom they blamed for their unhappiness or whom they regarded as lacking appropriate sympathy and understanding. We were also concerned that publication of a poem, for example, might confer a sense of permanency on work which, in subsequent years, the writers might wish they had not written. Thus, our preliminary discussions involved issues affecting past, present and future needs, and how we would edit the work we received. In the event much work has had, with agreement, to be discarded irrespective of its intrinsic interest or aesthetic merit.

After these preliminary discussions, staff at Barnardos undertook to explain to potential contributors what we wanted to achieve through writing the book: that is, to give them a voice (as people who have suffered at the hands of others) and also to assist care workers to help others in the future. It was made clear that the project would be a collaborative one: that is, the contributors would be co-authors with the editors. We then met with the groups of writers so that we could explain our personal backgrounds and the work we wanted to do; the writers were given the opportunity to ask any questions or voice any concerns they might have. Workers from the projects always sat in the groups. Key issues that had to be discussed in these meetings were confidentiality and anonymity. The writers then made the decision about whether they wanted to contribute to the book.

In the Open Door Project, the young people from the writers' group who wanted to participate were interviewed individually after the initial group meeting. Members of the children's group were already saying they wanted to participate even before they met us, as their worker had done a great deal of preparatory work with them. Interviews took place immediately after the initial meeting.

How materials were collected

1. Children and young people

The children and young people had already written their poems and stories. They were asked to consider what they would like included in the book. We then conducted a further interview with each contributor individually to ensure that we understood the various contexts of their writings (see below).

2. Individual adults

Individuals who had responded to our advertisements sent their poems and stories to us by post or email. Interviews were then conducted either face to face or by telephone. Similar interviews and discussions also took place with members of Beyond Existing.

3. Journals

Journal writing had been used as a method of working towards the healing process in the Beyond Existing groups. Two writers, Vera and Denise, agreed to their work being included in this book. While interviewing young people at the Reach Out Project, we discovered that Amanda and Jo had also written journals and were willing to share them with us.

4. Drawings

As we were collecting the materials, it became evident that many writers also produced drawings and artwork. We have included a few of these in this book, although the main focus remains on the use of creative writing in the healing process.

In short, we collected poems, stories, journals and drawings. These are presented in separate chapters and with separate commentaries (apart from the drawings, which are interspersed). During receipt of these materials, individual interviews were conducted. The content of these interviews is outlined below and the replies we received appear both in the context of the individual presentations and, more generally, in Chapter 4 (on Themes).

The interviews

Our interviews with all the writers were semi-structured around the following issues:

- what prompted them to start writing
- where, when and how they wrote
- what they did with their writing
- the context of each poem/story they had submitted for publication
- their views regarding the usefulness of writing groups
- advice they would give to workers who were thinking of using creative writing as a method of helping others who had suffered similar abusive situations.

Some writers found it very difficult to talk about themselves and their work; this highlighted the fact that writing was for them a vitally important medium through which to communicate. Others enjoyed talking. Consequently, the duration of interviews ranged from 25 minutes to two hours, with a mean of 47 minutes. Some writers who found it difficult to speak in interview subsequently wrote letters to us or sent emails to give more information because, as they said, they had thought more about the questions after interview.

The shape of the book and how the materials are used

After we had completed the interviews, it was evident that we had a wealth of materials that could be used. As some writers had given large quantities of work, they and we felt it would be helpful to put their favourite pieces in the main body of the book and their other work in a separate section, so that readers could use the materials as they wished in the future.

In conclusion, what is published here represents original material which has been selected by the writers themselves, both individually and collectively, and by those who carry responsibilities for their well-being. In our presentation of poetry, each contribution is prefaced by a brief outline of the circumstances surrounding its writing, the writer's views about its purpose and value, and then by editorial comments on its meaning and usefulness to the carer as a means of getting in touch with the feelings and needs of its writer.

Is there a theoretical basis to the whole work? As editors, we have attempted to avoid imposing any theoretical constructs, which might detract from the intentions of the writers. We do, however, believe that in certain circumstances, with certain people and with certain safeguards, creative writing is of intrinsic therapeutic value and can enlarge the understanding of care workers – provided, of course, that they can cope personally with the honesty and intensity (and sometimes the pain) of what is written.

In what ways can creative writing be regarded as a therapeutic experience in itself? Why do it? Why should it be encouraged? First, it can be cathartic, in that it provides a means of emotional relief from traumatic experiences. Second, it may enable the author to feel that he or she is taking control of bewildering life experiences by putting them in some sort of order; it enables him or her to be, and to feel, creative within what may otherwise be a chaos of feeling; it externalises inner pain, and puts it into a context of the past and the future. Third, it offers the opportunity of expressing what can loosely be called spiritual needs – needs that lie beyond the usual remit of the helping services.

One of our contributors, Sue, has written of the way in which writing provides her with this kind of therapeutic experience. She speaks of the 'physician' within herself as the primary (though not the only) source for resolving both her earlier pain and her need and hope for future healing:

Heal the Pain

To heal from pain
First let yourself feel it
Live with it
Explore its hidden depths.

To heal from pain
Share it
Like the seasons of your heart
The sun and the clouds.

To heal from pain

Accept it
As a part of you
Not to be ignored

To heal from pain
Be the physician
Within all of us
And heal your sick self.

To heal from pain
Trust the physician
Take the bitter potion
In silence and tranquillity.
To heal from pain
You must first know it.

A brief note at the end of this chapter (Appendix 1.1) guides the reader to recent publications which explain and exemplify these areas of therapeutic value. In the present work, our aims are more limited: giving a voice to the service-user, showing how this voice can contribute to assessments made by carers and showing how the carer's encouragement can enhance the healing process in situations of traumatic abuse.

As an introduction to these purposes, we have encouraged the social workers who set up the writing groups from which our contributors are drawn to outline how they approached the task, how the groups are organised, and the problems and satisfactions they have experienced. These accounts are set out in the following chapter, and form the framework of the writings which follow.

Two points need elaboration. First, source material on the therapeutic value of creative writing; second, the legal context of work in abusive situations. These are set out in the following appendices.

Appendix 1.1: The Therapeutic Value of Creative Writing

The publishers of this book have recently published other books which set out the usefulness of creative writing in a range of therapeutic contexts. We warmly recommend them to the reader as forming a contextual justification of this approach to helping others.

Gillie Bolton (1999) *The Therapeutic Potential of Creative Writing*. This provides a comprehensive overview of the various styles and contents of therapeutic writing. It offers useful guidance on how to set about writing, and how to teach others to set about it.

Deborah Philips, Liz Linington and Debra Penman (1999) *Writing Well: Creative Writing and Mental Health*. A guide to how to run a creative writing group for patients with mental health problems.

Celia Hunt and Fiona Sampson (eds) (1998) *The Self on the Page*. This study is a scholarly work with useful practical insights. In the first part, it demonstrates the use of writing with specific groups of service-users; and in the second part, it provides a theoretical basis for this form of therapy.

Appendix 1.2: The Legal Context of Work with Children and Adults

All work undertaken with children is guided by the Children Act 1989, and workers who may be encouraging creative writing need to be clear about their roles and responsibilities in undertaking such work where disclosure about abuse may be facilitated. All workers in contact with children should be aware of their responsibilities under the Children Act 1989. It is helpful to become familiar with government guidance in *Working Together to Safeguard Children* (DH, Home Office, Department of Education and Employment 1999) and *Framework for the Assessment of Children in Need and their Families* (DH *et al.* 2000).

The emphasis is on shared responsibility:

> Promoting children's well-being and safeguarding them from significant harm depends crucially upon effective information, sharing, collaboration and understanding between agencies and professionals.
>
> (DH et al. 1999, s.1.10, p.2)

The guidance goes on to state that:

> Somebody may abuse or neglect a child by inflicting harm, or by failing to act to prevent harm. Children may be abused in a family or in an institutional or community setting; by those known to them or, more rarely, by a stranger.
>
> (DH et al. 1999, s.2.3, p.5)

Under s.31(9) of the Children Act 1989:

> 'harm' means ill-treatment or the impairment of health or development; 'development' means physical, intellectual, emotional, social or behavioural development; 'health' means physical or mental health; and 'ill-treatment' includes sexual abuse and forms of ill-treatment which are not physical.

Categories of abuse include:

- physical
- emotional
- sexual
- neglect.

All workers are bound by the Children Act and, therefore, if a worker suspects that a child is being or has been abused they have a *duty to report*. It has to be made clear to any child that a worker cannot keep secrets. If a child discloses abuse during creative writing work, and the abuse has not previously been dealt with, the worker will have to report it. We shall show later in the book how it is imperative that workers set clear ground rules before working with a victim, whether child or adult.

Dealing with a vulnerable adult is less clear-cut as it is assumed that adults can make their own decisions unless deemed to lack mental capacity. Adult abuse has received less attention than child abuse. However, in 2000 there was a major development when the Department of Health issued *No Secrets: Guidance on Developing and Implementing Multi-agency Policies and Procedures to Protect Vulnerable Adults from Abuse* (DH 2000a). A Circular from the Department of Health stated:

> Directors of Social Services will be expected to ensure that the local multi-agency codes of practice are developed and implemented by 31 October 2001.
>
> (DH 2000b, p.2.)

Six categories of abuse were defined:

- physical
- sexual
- psychological
- financial or material
- neglect and acts of omission
- discriminatory.

> (DH 2000a, s.2.7, p.9)

'Abuse' itself is defined as follows:

> Abuse may consist of a single act or repeated acts. It may be physical, verbal or psychological, it may be an act of neglect or an omission to act, or it may occur when a vulnerable person is persuaded to enter into a financial or sexual transaction to which he or she has not consented, or cannot consent. Abuse can occur in any relationship and may result in significant harm to, or exploitation of, the person subjected to it.

(DH 2000a, s.2.6, p.9)

The definition of 'significant harm' was adopted from the Green Paper *Who Decides* (Lord Chancellor's Department 1997), which was based on the Children Act definition:

> ...not only ill treatment (including sexual abuse and forms of ill treatment which are not physical), but also the impairment of, or an avoidable deterioration in, physical or mental health; and the impairment of physical, intellectual, emotional, social or behavioural development.

(Lord Chancellor's Department 1997, s.8.11, p.68)

In recent years there has been increased usage of the term 'vulnerable adult'. However, it should be remembered that an adult may become vulnerable for different reasons at different points in life. For policy and procedural purposes, *No Secrets* defines a vulnerable adult as a person:

> who is or may be in need of community care services by reason of mental or other disability, age or illness; and who is or may be unable to take care of him or herself, or unable to protect him or herself against significant harm or exploitation.

(DH 2000a, s.2.3, pp.8–9)

It is imperative that any worker who intends to use creative working as a method of working with victims of abuse (child or adult) should familiarise themselves with, and have a thorough understanding of:

- definitions of abuse (as defined nationally and also locally) – i.e. child abuse, domestic violence, adult/elder abuse

- local policy and procedures regarding child protection, domestic violence and adult protection work
- roles and responsibilities in regard to reporting abuse
- local protocols for sharing information between agencies.

CHAPTER 3

The Projects

Chapter 2 explained how three projects became involved in contributing to this book. This chapter presents some background information about those projects in order to give the reader an insight into the environments which have offered the writers support and encouraged their creative writing.

Open Door Project

This project is based in a large early-Victorian terraced house in a northern industrial city. It is sponsored by Barnardos as part of a national initiative to help children who have been sexually abused, and those parents and other children who have directly or indirectly suffered or been involved in this problematic area of public concern. There is a team of seven members, assisted by several others who offer sessional help from time to time.

A wide range of services is available, and these reflect the use of several modes of intervention. In addition to therapeutic play-work for children, and counselling for people of all ages, the project has groups for children, young women, young men, art therapy, parents and partners, and other carers. Family therapy work is undertaken where abuse has occurred, in order to aid recovery and to ensure the children's future safety. Staff offer partnerships and consultancy services to other agencies, provide a variety of training courses and supervised practical experience for social work students, and contribute to the assessment of needs and risks on behalf of children and young people. Staff are active in trying and evaluating new approaches to the problems they meet, and in contributing to conferences and seminars nationally and abroad. The work is evaluated as an essential component *within* professional practice, and also externally by a local university.

Three groups are undertaking work of direct relevance to this book:

- a therapeutic writers' group of young people which uses creative writing as a means of recovery from the trauma of abuse

- two children's groups which produce individual and collective art, jointly written stories, and consequent opportunities to act out and resolve traumatic experiences.

Members of the groups have published their work as contributors to training and national conferences, and three young people from the first group and seven children from the second have participated in the preparation of this book.

It is difficult to encapsulate the principles that guide the wide range of activities within this project. Some of the most important are that:

- All work should be based on understanding what a traumatic situation means to the individual who experiences it; any behavioural problems are addressed by this route rather than tackled as the primary concern.

- Individual counselling and group activities are complementary in that they share the same recipients, the same purposes and the same values.

- All work should be time-focused: individual contracts are subject to regular review and revision; these are conducted with the service users and lead to agreed plans for the future.

- It is possible to help children to replace their post-traumatic chaotic behaviour by means of the development of group rituals and group-devised boundaries.

- Group *leaders* are essentially also group *members*; thus they need *overtly* to go in and out of role, particularly in work with children ('Who am I now?' 'This is Anna speaking now'), but safeguards are maintained regarding sharing personal information.

Reach Out Project

The writing group whose work contributes to this manual forms part of an open access and peer support service for 16 to 24-year-olds. It is a Barnardos project with additional local funding. The service is open all day, and often into the evenings, and provides:

- drop-in practical support, advice and advocacy
- groups offering social education
- a focus for young people with a range of special needs to campaign for improved services.

The service supports young people with a wide range of difficulties. About 30 per cent have mental health problems, and contact is maintained with those periodically admitted to hospital; several have anxieties about their sexuality; about half are homeless when they come to the service, often because of the break-up of their families or because they are escaping from physical or sexual abuse.

The service is based in a converted shop in a main street of a northern seaside town, and the building has three floors. Though the accommodation is limited for the amount of work currently undertaken, room has been found for a cafe, a creche, a computer room, a study space and a common room in addition to an administrative office and staffroom.

Creative work is encouraged. The young people devise all the publicity for the service, take part in presentations to other services (both nationally and locally) and produce the equipment they need. This is often highly imaginative: charts of things and situations they hate, large decorated bags for punching or hugging, bags in which they can take refuge from others, charts on which to record what they like about themselves or about others in the various groups.

In the year 2000–2001, about 500 young people used the services, and the range of their personal difficulties comprised self-harm, drug abuse, eating disorders and difficulties in sustaining relationships, as well as a variety of diagnosed mental disorders. Some used the service only fleetingly (the telephone, the cafe etc.), but for others the use is consistent, even daily.

The Reach Out Writing Group was set up at the direct request of service-users. It meets weekly and is facilitated by the deputy manager of the service – a woman with social work training and experience – and a man trained in youth work. They have worked together for about one and a half years. Four members have contributed to the present book, and a fifth member is a talented young artist who provides illustrations for members' writings and for their house magazine.

The aims of Reach Out, as devised by the members themselves, are:

- to share and support each other
- to have fun and a good laugh
- to let others know about their needs
- to challenge prejudice of all kinds.

But they have also devised certain ground rules:

- Always respect each other.
- Listen to others: it is okay to talk and equally okay to keep quiet.
- Preserve other people's confidences.
- Accept that members remain members even if they miss sessions.
- Get one's message across without shouting or swearing.

The group has already published two books of poetry and regularly produces a house magazine. They have been invited to several professional conferences and have taken part in several external research projects. The project is financially supported by local health and social services.

A recent evaluation of the project conducted by the Mental Health Foundation drew particular attention to the following achievements:

- the provision of a safe, accessible and supportive 'space'
- the group's acceptance of a wide range of needs

- the young people's capacity to control and develop the work of the group
- the ways in which members are empowered and gain in self-esteem by sharing their coping strategies, witnessing each other's experiences, learning to make informed choices, and learning to recognise their expertise in defining the nature of their mental health problems.

A visit to the group indicates how far the project leaders have successfully blurred the traditional distinction made between those who provide help and those who receive it.

Essentially, both the Reach Out work and the project as a whole are based on principles that are specifically geared to the promotion of mental health and to giving unconditional respect to all those who seek help. These principles have been summarised by members in the box on the following page.

Thomas, one of the members, has summarised their work as follows:

Reach Out

Mental health concern at this base
We could have it at another place
We've been doing it for a few weeks now
Why we do it, don't ask me how

We just set up for young people
Who wanted to feel alright and not feeble
So come along even if you feel lost
You can get your message across.

From the standpoint of the facilitators, the principal rewards of the project have been the high level of mutual support among the young people, and the ways in which they are able to share their coping strategies, both in direct relationships with each other and in their writings. Sometimes they help each other in very practical ways, like making beanbags for hugging and punching when individual stresses become acute. They have worked together in making presentations about mental health services to training courses and, notably, to one of Anthony Clare's programmes in the *All in the Mind* series on Radio 4, and to 200 delegates at the Brighter Futures Conference organised by the Mental

Respectful

Reception   Young people need to be treated as individ-
                      uals, not diagnosed, being welcomed and
                      accepted from the moment they access a
                      project.

Encouragement   Our work should be about encouragement,
                      to maximise what young people can do,
                      achieve, cope with.

Support   Not being blamed if they need support, but
                      given it in a way they can accept.

Power   Maximising the power and control they
                      have within the group/sessions and
                      projects. Realistically empowering them.
                      Mental health often means
                      disempowerment.

Education   Opportunities for education, to try again,
                      explore options. Education about their
                      mental health problems, letting them
                      educate us about their view of their diffi-
                      culties.

Care   True care, empathy, warmth. In all ways we
                      can show care.

Time   Giving people enough time, and at a time
                      they need it, not when we want to give it.

Fun   Having fun is good for everyone's mental
                      health and is an important way of sharing
                      in other people's lives. Prioritise it.

Unique   Each person is unique and needs to be
                      treated and valued as such.

Laughter   Time for laughter. It's worth a thousand
                      pills and hours of therapy.

(From the Reach Out Project: 2000)

Health Foundation. Inevitably, however, there are 'lows' when members temporarily lose their motivation because of the emergence of new personal stresses; the death of a member was a time of great distress for everyone. But the existence of the group as a vehicle for urgent self-expression provides a lifeline for members who, singly, could not cope with severe emotional difficulties.

Beyond Existing

The beginning

Beyond Existing is an organisation that runs support groups for adults who have been abused. It was set up in May 2000 as a result of a research project which had been funded by the Joseph Rowntree Foundation: *The Needs of Older Women: Services for Victims of Elder Abuse and Other Abuse* (Pritchard 2000). The main objective of the original project, which was undertaken in three social services departments, was to identify the needs of older women who had been victims of elder abuse. It was recognised that some of them may have also experienced abuse in childhood and earlier adulthood and therefore the project aimed to identify any needs resulting from previous abusive experiences. The focus of inquiry broadened to include older men, when male victims of elder abuse started to disclose to the researcher (Pritchard 2001).

When the findings of the research project were fed back in focus groups to the original interviewees, many of them enjoyed meeting each other and said that it would be helpful to meet with other victims of abuse on a regular basis in order to get further support. The Joseph Rowntree Foundation agreed to fund a pilot study, which ran initially for six months. After evaluating the pilot study Beyond Existing continued because victims did find support groups a positive intervention in helping them to heal from abuse experienced recently or in the past.

Objectives

After the first year, Beyond Existing started to receive requests for younger adults to be involved in a group. It was decided to broaden Beyond Existing's remit to include all vulnerable adults:

The term 'vulnerable adult' includes any male or female over the age of 18 years who may have a physical, sensory or learning disability, a mental health problem or who is an older person.

       (3.1. Beyond Existing Constitution, January 2003)

The forms of abuse experienced by the adults, whether in childhood or adulthood, are defined as:

The term 'abuse' will include physical, emotional, financial, neglect, sexual and discriminatory. Abuse may be referred to as harm, mis-treatment, or exploitation.

       (3.2 Beyond Existing Constitution, January 2003)

The main aims of Beyond Existing have been to:

- Convene support groups which will provide practical and emotional help and aid recovery from the long-term effects of abuse.

- Make support groups available to vulnerable adults who have been abused either in childhood or adulthood.

- Offer support and practical advice to any vulnerable adult who has either left the abusive situation or who may still be experiencing abuse.

- Offer vulnerable adults understanding of their experiences of abuse, the causes of abuse and how to deal with abusive situations. Training will also be offered to promote self-esteem and a sense of well-being, e.g. assertiveness training, literacy skills, the help available from other services etc.

Who attends

In a three-year period, Beyond Existing has run three support groups for adults aged between 29 and 93 years:

1. Quarry Group – older people; men and women (June 2000–June 2001)

2.   Calder Group – older people; all women (June 2000–June 2001)

3.   Morrison Group – younger and older adults with learning disabilities and mental health problems; all women (October 2001 ongoing).

The 21 adults who attended the groups have experienced abuse in their lifetime as:

Child abuse	8	(38%)
Domestic violence	10	(48%)
Adult/elder abuse	19	(90%)

The work of Beyond Existing has been written up in detail elsewhere (Pritchard 2003).

Location

When the findings of the original research project were published fictitious names were used for the three social services departments who had participated. Beyond Existing was set up in one of these areas, which is known as Churchtown. The members live within a large county in the North of England. It is of paramount importance to keep members of the groups safe and the venue used for the meetings is never publicised. It will suffice to say that the groups have met in a local authority resource centre, where older people can have respite care (perhaps while rehabilitating) and day care is also provided. The resource centre is located just outside a city centre. It is a modern two-storey building which is well decorated and bright. There are three lounges on the ground floor, one of which is used by Beyond Existing for meetings. Upstairs the day centre and bedrooms are located, together with the therapy rooms. A local social service area office adjoins the back of the building.

The use of creative writing

Various methods of communication have been used in the groups to facilitate members' progress through the healing process. Two such methods have been (1) engaging in written exercises and (2) using creative writing. The work undertaken in the groups brought about the idea for this book (see Chapter 1) and as a result members of the groups have made a huge contribution to this publication.

CHAPTER 4

Themes from the Interviews with the Writers

In Chapter 2, there was a brief outline of our objectives in interviewing the writers who had agreed to contribute to this book. Our interest lay in discovering the various contexts within which they wrote, and thus to understand a little better what their writing meant to them and how it fitted into their lives. During the course of these interviews certain themes started to emerge and it is the purpose of this chapter to present and discuss them. In the first instance, we need to remember what the writers had in common:

- They all had experienced abuse of some kind, principally physical or sexual.

- They all had at some point received (or were still receiving) services from statutory or voluntary agencies.

- They all wrote poetry, stories or journals as a means of expressing their feelings: that is to say, writing was not simply for fun.

Verbal expression

What became evident in interview was that many of the writers had difficulty in expressing themselves spontaneously. This applied both within and outside the interviews. One would expect reticence in talking about the abuse they had experienced to two strangers, but many found difficulty in talking about their writing. It became apparent that for some their self-esteem was extremely low (a common long-term effect of abuse) and they did not think their writing was worthy of publication:

> I hate most of it. Don't think it's much good.
>
> *Alex*

> When people keep saying you're useless for a long time you end up believing it. I believe it now.
>
> *Thomas*

Consequently, some of the interviews were short because the writers found it difficult to talk about their work. This was a common theme among both younger and older adults, and it emphasises the importance of writing as a medium of self-expression. If victims cannot talk about what has happened to them, then it is vital that they find another way of expressing their feelings at the time of the abuse and when receiving therapeutic help.

Not being believed

One of the difficulties in verbal comunication may link partly to a mistrust of people and to the common fear (for many victims of abuse) that they will not be believed. All the writers had experienced abuse, some from a very early age – Laura had been two years old when the abuse started. Some writers talked about telling their mothers about the abuse and not being believed:

> I told me mam and she didn't believe me. I told my auntie.
>
> *Sinead*

> She ignored it. Nothing will change her mind.
>
> *Beccy*

Alex was abused again after she was admitted to residential care; when she told social workers about this she was not believed:

> I told them but they said I was a liar. It happened for a year before they moved me.

Services from professionals

All the writers had experience of receiving services from a wide range of professionals and workers: social worker, residential care worker, project worker, psychiatrist, community psychiatric nurse, counsellor, police. In addition, several had been admitted into the care of the local authority at the age stated in brackets and volunteered various ideas about this:

> Amanda (7)
> Alex (8)
> Beccy (14)
> Jo (6)
> Sinead (10)
> Thomas (15)

Others had been in care but did not raise this in interview.

As one would expect, the writers had mixed experiences and feelings about the services they received. Some were critical of social workers in particular:

> Can't stand them [social workers].
>
> *Alex*

> I hate [social worker]. She made me wait to see my little brother.
>
> *Sinead*

Others were critical of professionals in general:

> They should not be high and mighty. They need to be down to earth. Don't be snobby. Need to think like you… Don't tar everyone with the same brush. They make judgements.
>
> *Jo*

Thomas was critical about the number of workers who had been assigned to him; in the past year he had had three different workers from the same community mental health team:

> They have not been very helpful. You get used to one person. You get comfortable with them. Then they leave.

He also felt that the psychiatrist did not listen to him when he was having problems with the medication he was taking:

I didn't like the way he was with me… I felt the medication was not helping me. I was told to give it time and was kept on it. Eventually the psychiatrist left.

Amanda was also critical of psychiatrists:

They ask you to do stupid pictures.

She was very proud of the fact that she had managed to take herself off anti-depressants without any support from the professionals.

Beccy had had a particularly bad experience after she disclosed information about abuse to the police. She was told that she had done the right thing in telling the truth, but when she thought she was going home from the police station, she was taken directly into local authority care. She felt it had all been arranged secretly. Beccy also talked about how she had kept a diary when she first came into care. The police broke the lock off her diary and it was used as evidence against the foster parent who abused her. The diary was given back to her after the court case; she threw it away and has never kept a diary since.

Beccy also criticised the professionals for being dishonest. When she read her files after leaving care, she found that a psychiatrist had put her on valium without her knowledge. She had been told that the tablets were chalk because she had a chalk deficiency (which she has not).

Counselling had been provided to a number of the writers; some had started writing because it had been suggested by their counsellors. However, some had found that the counsellor was not reciprocally helpful or supportive. Sue had written a journal for her counsellor, who was part of an NHS Mental Health Team; but the counsellor refused to keep the journal safe for her and Sue still feels very bitter about this. She consequently destroyed the journal in anger but now regrets this:

If they [the victims] are willing to share, they are sharing the deepest part of them and you should respect that…

Sue later said that any worker supporting someone through writing should:

Talk to the person. Ask what they want. Keep the writing. Read it. Give it back. You cannot do with it what you want.

Indie Larma was similarly critical of the way her counsellor had used her writing. She said she enjoyed talking about her poetry with the counsellor at first, but then:

> She started leading me down the wrong path. Putting words in my mouth. She was putting her own interpretation on the work. She did the analysing, not me... She was very unprofessional. I ended up counselling her.

It was as a result of receiving poor services that some of the writers have since taken steps to gain qualifications in social care or have ambitions to follow a career path in welfare services:

> I could do it properly because I have seen so many bad ones [social workers].
>
> *Beccy*

Beccy is currently studying for a Diploma in Social Work and Sue is training to be a counsellor. Gemma wants to work in child protection within the police service and in the meantime she is involved in helping with the children's writing group in the Open Door Project; Alex wants to work for the NSPCC. Other writers, Indie Larma and Laura, are currently working in the caring professions.

However, not all the comments made about services and workers were negative. The children and younger adults who were still involved with the Open Door and Reach Out Projects explained how they could talk to the workers in these projects:

> He really listens.
>
> *Jo*

> Social workers demand that you talk to them but the [Open Door workers] wait for you to say.
>
> *Alex*

Gemma was very positive about the support she had received from the police even though her case did not proceed to court:

> I felt devastated. But the police said they believed me but it came down to my word against [the abuser].

Starting to write

The writers started writing in varying circumstances and at very different ages. Some (for example, Alex, Indie Larma, Denise) had started as a direct response to a professional worker suggesting that this might be a way of working therapeutically; others had always enjoyed writing and wrote about their abusive experiences regularly and frequently at certain times in their lives. For example, Gemma wrote much between the ages of 11 and 13 and at 15; for Sue most writing was done in her early teens, twenties and thirties. For others, starting to write was a direct and spontaneous reaction to not receiving support:

> At 14 I had problems and tried to talk to people but no one would listen to me.
>
> *Jo*

Beccy started writing at the age of 14. A friend started sending poetry to her, so she wrote back. Thomas started writing poetry when he entered a poetry competition at school when he was 15 years old. He won the competition and then started writing and winning quite regularly:

> I was not good at explaining how I felt. It's a way of expressing my feelings.

Amanda only started writing a year ago after a project worker:

> …said I should start. I mainly do it when I feel down in the dumps. When I can't be bothered with anyone else.

Vera remembers that:

> It all started with a dream about the Lofthouse mining disaster. My ex-husband had to wake me up. I had seen in the dream a man wearing orange in water. Within two weeks I had the urge to write.

Laura found that when she was working professionally with a paedophile, this triggered memories of her own abuse:

> I'd never written before. Just felt like doing it one day.

Purpose of writing

One of the most important objectives in interviewing the writers was to ask them why they wrote, and the purpose of their creative writing. Some of the quotations above have clearly indicated that writing is a way of venting feelings which cannot be expressed in speech. For some it was a medium through which they could 'talk' to their abuser:

> I wrote what I wanted to say to my Dad and couldn't.
>
> *Sue*

> I thought I'll piss people off. I'll get back at them. It was like I was saying it to them. All the things I couldn't say.
>
> *Beccy*

In short some were writing to help themselves by ventilating anger; but some were very clear that it was also beneficial in 'reflecting back' in order to move through the healing process:

> You can see how you've moved on.
>
> *Alex*

> It's better to get something off your mind. Then it's left.
>
> *Gemma*

Vera wrote for others as well as for herself:

> I wrote them for myself with a thought for other people who needed to know how to stop being miserable... [Writing] always seems to start on a low and finish up on a high.

Gemma talked about how writing could help victims to disclose their needs:

> Some people may be too embarrassed to tell workers. Writing can be a way of telling.

Thomas told us that his objective in writing poetry was to 'talk' to people when he did not know how they felt about him; it was his way of making contact and finding out other people's thoughts about himself. It came across in interview that it is important for Thomas to know what people think about him because he is very self-conscious of having Tourette Syndrome.

Amanda was very open about the fact she often feels suicidal and she talks about death a great deal. Writing helps her get through each day:

[Writing] helps us. Gets stuff out of you – the shit out of you. Another day goes... I get agitated very easily. I could easily die tomorrow – even today.

When they wrote

The writers were asked *when* they wrote. As already discussed, some wrote when they were feeling particularly low, depressed, when people would not listen or in a response to a particular problem. A frequent theme was writing when they were alone late at night:

Late at night – three or four in the morning.

Thomas

Mostly at night when I was upset and on my own.

Beccy

In the early hours.

Sue

For others, writing was done in response to an urgent need:

When I am angry I scribble, I draw – mad feelings. I write in a frenzy. Takes about fifteen minutes.

Jo

You feel when something is coming.

Indie Larma

Vera tended to write in the middle of the night, but she differed from others in that she did not write immediately after specific suffering:

I never wrote when I was attacked by my husband but always long after the event.

Sue wrote 'a lot – continually' when her father (the abuser) was terminally ill.

Where they wrote

Writers were asked *where* they wrote. Indie Larma and Amanda were the only two writers who could write in both private and in public places:

I write at home and at work.

Indie Larma

I can write anywhere.

Amanda

Everyone else wrote in private – in their bedrooms, living rooms or on the floor in the corner of the bedroom.

As the writing was often spontaneous, as a reaction to feelings, most writers just grabbed pieces of paper that were within reach – 'bits of paper', 'scrap', 'blank sheets of paper found at ends of books' – and they wrote by hand. Vera, however, wrote in a red exercise book. Beccy always wrote on A4 paper. Some chose to transcribe their work into a book at a later date (Jo) or to type up their work later (Amanda, Alex). Only Laura, when she decided to write her story (see Chapter 8), used a computer, though Alex said she now uses a computer because of arthritis in her hands.

How long the writing took

This varied considerably; many wrote very quickly as soon as an idea came into their heads, and made few alterations:

Half an hour at the most.

Gemma

Lines come into my head. I write it down straight away…up to half an hour.

Jo

Probably took twenty minutes. Hardly altered anything once it was written down. It was spontaneous.

Indie Larma

Others lingered over their writing or spent a considerable length of time at their task:

Sometimes I can sit and write for hours and write loads.

Alex

At one point Thomas used to write every day. On one occasion he wrote 60 poems in eight hours. Vera's method of writing poetry was somewhat different:

> I start and go back to them – two or three months later. If it didn't sound right – it had to rhyme and connect with the lines above it – I would delete it if it was wrong.

In addition to writing poems, Vera, Denise, Jo and Amanda also used journals (see Chapter 7). Vera used her journal every day like a diary to express her feelings whereas, as noted earlier, her poems were more reflective; most entries were short, so the writing did not take very long. Denise wrote extensively when a crisis occurred and would then spend a considerable time writing her journal.

Storing the writing

It was important to the writers to keep the writing safe and private. A common theme was that the writing should be hidden. Places mentioned included: a special folder, bedroom drawers, underneath the bed, in the bedside table, in a schoolbag, in a safe locked place.

Indie Larma described in detail what she did with her writing:

> I would fold the bits of paper after writing the poems and hide them in different places. I did not want anyone to find them and no one ever looks in piles of magazines and other rubbish piled high. Eventually I started putting them in a big red book because I did not want to lose what I had written. I had also tried to use this red book as a journal but it did not work for me. I felt if the writing ever went missing it would be like losing part of me. I now keep them in a bookcase.

> At one time I carried it around so that no one would see it.

Sue

Destroying work

Some writers talked about destroying their work; we have already mentioned the fact that Sue destroyed her work when she was angry with her counsellor. Laura had been given a notebook by her counsellor:

I wrote a lot of rubbish. I didn't keep it.

Alex said she had 'binned' a lot of her work, but the project workers persuaded her to keep a lot of other work which she had been going to throw out. There were various reasons for destroying work: as a spontaneous expression of anger or disgust; as a symbolic way of putting paid to the past and, at best, looking to the future; or because of dissatisfaction or shame about what had been written. There was no unifying theme on this matter.

Frequency of writing

Laura has only ever written one poem and one story; Steven had written only one poem. Some wrote at certain critical periods in their lives and then stopped (Gemma and Thomas). Some have stopped and then started again (the longest period Vera stopped for was three years). Others continue to write. The type of writing also changed for some writers: some wrote poetry and then went on to stories; others kept diaries and then went on to poetry. Gemma and Beccy both wish to write a book. Gemma wanted to write a book about what had happened to her, and a local journalist was interested in helping her to get it published, but:

> I became scared and backed out. I started thinking 'What would people think?' I'm so young. I also wanted it to be private.

Beccy has started to write her book:

> I have written part of my 'life story'. I started writing this when I decided to make a success of my life, when I was 22. I've only gotten to the part when I went into care because I only write about four times a year. After I'm qualified I plan to get it published some day, that's my dream anyway.

Feelings and sharing

The writers were asked how they felt *after* they had written something. A common response was 'relief'. But there were other reactions too:

> Howled for hours. Then I'd go back and say 'Blimey did I really do that?' It was almost as though it was two different people.
>
> *Indie Larma*

Maintaining privacy seemed to be a common theme among all the writers, but we were interested to know whether they ever shared their work and with whom. All the writers clearly understood the purpose of this present book: that is, to help workers understand the needs of victims of abuse and how creative writing might be used to help them. Therefore, it was important for the writers to tell us *how* creative writing can be used helpfully by workers. The common theme in response to this was that work would only be shared with people whom they trusted and felt safe with. The people specifically mentioned included: daughter, friends, project workers, tutor at school, line manager, counsellor. It was significant that only one or two recipients were mentioned in each reply except for those belonging to writing groups. Sue said she had only shared her work in recent years:

> with people who would gain from it. One person who had been abused, and another I suspected had experienced abuse.

Beccy talked about the positive responses she had from a community psychiatric nurse when she shared her poetry:

> She said I was talented and she understood more about me from reading [the poetry] than what I said to her.

Laura's sharing of her work had a beneficial effect for other victims of abuse:

> I never shared with anyone except my line manager who used them in her own work.

Writers who had worked in groups talked about the advantages of sharing in a writers' group.

> It's nice to share things.
>
> *Gemma*

> At times it is dead intense and erupts. You feel part of it. Everybody tries to help one another. It's like a community family.
>
> *Jo*

Sinead and Emma talked about what it had been like to work in the girls' group:

I felt a bit scared at first. I did not want to show my feelings. After, I felt happy and I really wanted to show my feelings.

Sinead

I liked making friends. You can talk to each other. Understand what they have been through. I came in sad, went out happy.

Emma

Self-harm

When discussing feelings it is necessary to talk about self-harm, which was mentioned by several writers. Self-harm needs to be distinguished from the threat or actuality of suicide. Some writers had made deliberate attempts at suicide or had deliberately overdosed. Others have harmed themselves in the past or continue to do so now. Paradoxical though it may seem, self-harm was not regarded by the writers we interviewed as necessarily a wholly negative act; it was therefore different from attempted suicide in this respect. For some, it was seen (and experienced) as a positive act because it was accompanied by a sense of release:

> Although self-injury has its own very specific meanings for an individual, the problems and motivations beneath self-injury are often similar to those underlying other, more familiar sorts of self-harm. For example, in the same way that one person may use drugs or drink to escape their feelings, so another may be able to distract herself from her emotional pain by hurting her body.
>
> (Arnold and Babiker 1998, p.135)

For some writers there was a clear link between the activity of writing and engaging in self-harm. Sue said that she writes immediately before and after harming herself: 'It is part of the process.' She cuts, burns, uses scrubbing brushes to cleanse herself. Jo said that sometimes writing the poetry would 'set off the self-harm'; she self-harms 'not regularly but often'.

In the past Beccy had self-harmed, overdosed several times and made one serious attempt at suicide when she was 19. She talked about how the writing helped her to stop herself from self-harming:

I self-harmed when I was upset. I would write poetry as suicide notes and then feel better. I stopped self-harming not through therapy or seeing someone, but gradually stopped myself by writing. Instead of self-harming I wrote.

Advice to potential writers

We asked each writer what advice they would give to potential writers:

Try to be happy and get on with your life. Show your feelings at anytime you want.

Sinead

Sit and think about what you want to get across.

Gemma

Ask for help.

Alex

Go to the library as there are lots of books of poems. Read famous people.

Thomas

Go with the flow. Doesn't matter about swearing. Write about what you want to write about. It might look a mess. Work on it. Use short sentences then put them in order and together.

Jo

Instead of thinking it – write it. The words will come.

Vera

Just sit down and write whatever comes into your head. I don't know what the connection is between head and hand.

Sue

Don't worry about what you write… If you are going to change things it is not going to happen in a moment.

Indie Larma

Before you write anything you have to accept your feelings.

Beccy

Advice to workers

It was also important to ask the writers what advice they would give to workers who were interested in using creative writing when working on a one-to-one basis or in groups:

Give them comfort. Make them happy.

Sinead

Not to push people. Let them bring stuff. They pick and choose what they want to share.

Gemma

Listen.

Alex, Amanda

You don't want people to take the piss [i.e. the group members]. They need to take the group seriously. One thing I hate is when workers say about what you've been through 'I know how you feel'... Workers should have been through the same experiences. Share their feelings. Set targets. Support each other and acknowledge each other.

Jo

Anything the person writes should not be changed. Should not be tamed. It should be rough around the edges, that is, the writing portrays the true feelings; the feelings are raw... Don't lead people. It's quicker if you let them do their own exploring. There's no quick fix. It's slow and gradual... You cannot dictate when people want to talk.

Indie Larma

Beccy talked at length about *how* workers had talked to her in a patronising way and that certain phrases were used frequently; for example: 'There's nothing you can tell me that I haven't heard before, so I won't be shocked' or 'I know how you feel'. She made it abundantly clear that these are not helpful responses.

Writing linked to other arts/skills

This book is about creative writing but many of the writers had other artistic skills. Thomas had originally been trying to write songs 'but left it to write poems'. During interview, some writers showed us the drawings they had done at the same time as writing, and many drawings were included in the written work. Some have been included in this book to show the link between writing and drawing. The next few pages show some of the drawings Jo produced while she wrote.

Figure 4.1 Jo's drawing 1

An interim comment

These themes have been presented in order to highlight the contexts in which the writers have produced their creative work, and within which we can better understand what (and why and how) they have written. It is, of course, true that what they have written – particularly their poems – could simply be read as creations wholly independent of the personalities of the writers; conventional literary appreciation is rooted in an acceptance of this separation, and some of the work presented here has undoubted literary merit in its own right.

But for our writers, what they are and what they experience cannot be divorced from what they have written, and vice versa; for the therapeutic value of their work depends on recognising the interdependence of creativity, past experiences and current emotional needs. The poems especially should not read *simply* as literary creations: they exist for important personal and private purposes.

On this assumption, therefore, we offer some general suggestions about how the poetry (and, to a lesser extent, the other writings) might usefully be approached.

How to read a poem

We were interested to find that, when it is suggested to service-users that they write about their difficult experiences or current distress, they most often choose to write poems. Why is this? Most obviously, there must be characteristics in the nature of poetry that match the need to encapsulate and record complex emotions. The *Oxford English Dictionary* (OED) gives some clues to what these things are: its definition of poetry includes the following ideas:

- metrical language or an equivalent patterned arrangement

- figurative uses and the option of syntactical order, differing from those of ordinary speech or prose writing

- language adapted to stir the imagination and emotions, both immediately and also through the harmonic suggestions latent in or implied by the words used.

We can take these ideas one by one and apply them to the experiences and writings included in this manual. First, poetry requires some sort of orderliness in the mind of the writer, by imposing a metrical form or some other kind of patterning. When writing a poem, one is constrained by metre or rhyme or form, and cannot therefore just 'rabbit on' as one can in other kinds of writing. As the poet Ezra Pound remarked, poetry is saying something important in the shortest possible way. For many of our contributors, though not all, the necessity of *orderly* writing paralleled and supported their need to transform their traumatic experiences into a manageable and therefore controllable form. The same process applies, of

Figure 4.2 Jo's drawing 2

course, to poetry written about overwhelming experiences of joy; but
sadly we are not concerned here with writers whose lives hitherto have
been joyful ones. It is significant, however, that when their feelings or
thoughts overflow the boundaries of rational discourse, many writers
turn to poetry, which provides them with a sense of freedom by exchang-
ing the constraints of logic for the constraints of form. As Matthew
Arnold said, in his essay on the poet Thomas Gray, 'Genuine poetry is
conceived and composed in the soul' – i.e. not in the reason or the wit.
(He undoubtedly overstates this, but one can see what he means.) A
striking example of this phenomenon occurs in St Paul's letter to the
Philippians in which, in the overwhelming wonder and joy of his
message, he breaks into poetry (Philippians 2: 6–11), and thereby
provides the Christian church with one of its earliest creeds and one of its
earliest hymns. In this manual, several writers rely on the discipline of
rhyme to force their minds into therapeutic orderliness. Others apparently 'let it all hang out' in emotional terms – sometimes writing at
enormous speed and without apparent discipline. But consider how

Figure 4.3 Jo's drawing 3

much more paper they would have needed to use to convey the same message in prose.

The second idea from the OED concerns the figurative uses of words, and freedom from normal syntax, as aspects of poetry. Poetry permits – even encourages – the use of metaphor, the hinting of events which do not need to be fully described; allusions to things which had better not be put into words because words would be too horrific or too painful; 'a sight to dream of, not to tell'. Several of the poems included here are concerned with childhood experiences of sexual abuse, described not in the forensic language of the courts but the allusive language of 'the soul'.

Figure 4.4 Jo's drawing 4

This links to the third idea in the dictionary definition: the language of poetry not only stirs our feelings now but, because of the intrinsic allusions and harmonies of the words used, we are likely to remember what we have read and learned; to live with it for a time, just as the writer has lived with it for an even longer period.

If we receive a poem from someone who has had bad experiences, we need, therefore, to be alert to certain requirements in our response:

- First, the person would not have written the poem if he or she could have told us face to face all the things that needed to be said; one does not need to write poems if everyday language can say it all.

- Second, the poem will hint at more things than it clearly states; it is not our job to probe like a forensic lawyer for more information, but rather to acknowledge that something important is being said which is difficult to put into words and which is perhaps a matter for *silent* sharing.

- Third, if writing the poem has served its purpose, the writer may now wish to set it aside as 'finished business'; several writers represented here have destroyed many more poems than they have kept, because the writing has done its healing work and they have now moved on to the next step in problem solving. On receiving a poem, therefore, a great deal of sensitivity is needed in knowing when to 'hark back' and when to 'let it lie'. Sensitivity of this kind cannot be taught, but it can be learnt.

William Wordsworth wrote in his Preface to the second edition of the *Lyrical Ballads* (1802), 'Poetry is the spontaneous overflow of powerful feelings: it takes its origin from emotion recollected in tranquillity.' There can be no doubt about the powerful feelings in the work presented here. In some of it, one is more aware of 'spontaneous overflow' than of 'tranquillity'. Certainly, some poems were written when the authors' only tranquillity was a brief time of quiet – usually at night – and writing what we can now read. But our writers would, in general, agree with Wordsworth's comments. Significantly, when we asked them to select the poems that they wished included here, they chose those to which they had given most thought or whose composition had been carefully revised. As mentioned earlier, many of the spontaneous heat-of-the-moment poems had been destroyed. They had served their purpose and were no longer 'relevant'. Where possible, we have tried to give examples of an author's spontaneity and of their subsequent recollection 'in tranquillity'.

Is there a risk in this process that the spontaneous expression of feelings will become an end in itself, a form of perpetual self-pity, a self-indulgent wallowing? Yes, there is. If these poems – and, indeed, other writings – are to have therapeutic validity, they should be regarded as steps towards a happier future, or at least towards a higher level of self-realisation. We have implied above that most writers recognise this – in destroying earlier work no longer needed, or in guiding us away from its publication. So if one is given a poem to read, it is appropriate to ask whether the author feels that the writing was helpful: did it feel like a step forward? Does he or she feel the need to write on precisely the same matter again, or are there new things to say?

It is perhaps useful to consider the parallel issue (of self-pity and self-indulgence) in the practice of counselling. Experience shows that if a counsellor *merely* encourages the ventilation of feelings over a period of several weeks and does not involve the client in thoughts about the possibilities of change, then the client's depression may deepen rather than reduce. The need for periodic stocktaking in counselling reflects the tendency in both counsellor and client to lose the capacity for positive change (and even to lose some of the positives already achieved) because of the almost hypnotic power of expressed feelings, *unless* joint stocktaking and a review of plans takes place, and a new impetus is found for working together. Some helpers are more skilled at helping people to ventilate their feelings than to engage in planning for the future; this is a tendency against which we all need to be on our guard.

All this can be applied to the business of encouraging and responding to creative writing. Writing has a purpose, but can fulfil that purpose only if it forms part of the sequence of steps leading to a sense of being healed, a sense of increased well-being and hope, and the achievement of more satisfactory social functioning.

It is apparent among our contributors that younger writers often present more impulsive work than older writers, whose poems are more obviously structured and thoughtful. We should expect this: the nearer we are to adolescence, the likelier we are to react abruptly to the apparent hopelessness of our situation; the older we are, the more we tend to be reflective. The sense of hopelessness may be just as strong, but we have learnt to live with it. This capacity for reflection means that the recipient of the poem is on safer ground when discussing it with the writer and, in interview, moving from the expression of feelings to planning for the future. But whatever the writer's age, we need to remember that the poem probably hints at greater distress than the words themselves define; we cannot ever be certain that we really understand the *intensity* of need but neither should we be overzealous in trying to find out.

CHAPTER 5

Using Poetry 1: Poems Presented by the Younger Adults

The following poems have been selected by their authors for presentation here. Their work is preceded by brief profiles of their personal circumstances, and we have added comments on how the poems might be understood. As editors, we are conscious that we may not have grasped all the implications of individual poems; we would hesitate to talk about our 'interpretation' of the poems. But we hope we have written enough to indicate how these works may be usefully approached. (No editing has been imposed on the poems themselves, except where it was necessary to avoid misunderstanding.)

Profile of Jo

Jo is 19 years old and currently living in bed and breakfast accommodation. She had just found out that she was pregnant when she was interviewed.

Jo has experienced physical, mental, emotional and sexual abuse and has been raped three times. She said one of the main issues for her was 'Mum and Dad beating us [Jo and sister] up'. She left when she was 12 years old because she was sexually abused by her adoptive brother. She has two adoptive brothers but 'only counts one as a brother'.

Jo first started writing when she was attending boarding school at the age of 14. She was going through a lot of problems at the time. She tried to talk to people but 'no one would listen to me'. She felt she was bullied by several people – teachers, care staff and in particular the female headteacher, who would 'humiliate me in front of the whole assembly'.

Jo has been attending the Reach Out Project for between one and a half and two years.

Update from Jo herself

'I am now living with foster carers. I am seven weeks off having my daughter. I am really happy with life now. I stopped self-harming at Christmas. I stopped taking drugs, smoking and drinking when I found out I was pregnant. I love both my daughter and life.'

The following five poems were among those selected by Jo for publication. They were written over a period of about two years, during which Jo attended the Reach Out Project. The first four poems express great unhappiness, but we have put them in an order that indicates a dim but growing sense of hope. We cannot be sure of the order in which they were written, but are confident that the first two represent her earliest work after joining the project; they show serious depression and a preoccupation with death. One senses that, for Jo at this time, time itself had come to a halt, and that there was therefore no way forward for her. The inextricable links between time and movement are worth noting: if time stops, there can be no movement; if one is feeling even mildly depressed, time drags.

Down, Down, Rope, Die!!

I'm all alone,
In this world,
I sit in my room,
Deep in my depression.

I can't see anyway forward,
And everything's so bleak,

I wish someone could get in my head,
Just to see how desperate I feel.

I just want to die,
Die and be free.
And then I start to cry,
And it lasts for ages.

Now I'm really low,
And I've tied the rope around my neck.
I leave it there for hours.
And now I can't breathe GOOD.
DIE BITCH DIE

I don't wish to speak,
I have nothing to say,
The hurt overcomes me,
So much I can't think.

I want to cry but can't,
And it drives me insane,
I wish I could die,
Coz of all the pain I'm in.

When Will It Be Over?

There's a devil inside,
But why is it here,
I want it to stop controlling me,
Stop controlling my head.

The nightmares I want them to end.
I'm afraid to go to sleep.
If I go to sleep,
I'll get stuck there forever.

People look at me in disgust.
But they haven't got a clue.
Why should they,
They don't care.

One day it'll all be over.
But until then,
I'll just have to do what he says,
And I'll keep cutting away till then.

One notes in these poems that Jo was unable to express and explain her desperation to other people: 'I wish someone could get in my head.' She cannot express her feelings by crying: some despair lies beyond tears. In these poems, death is seen as a way out from despair; or, at least, it will reduce despair sufficiently to be able to cry, to express feelings openly. When, in death, she can start to cry, 'it lasts for ages'.

The second poem is equally despairing and ends with the threat of serious self-harm; but there is a slight positive movement in so far as the depression has become partly objectified as the devil inside. In a sense, depression has become her second self rather than her whole self. She recognises the presence of other people (verse 3), but doubts their honest acceptance of her and their apparent friendliness. She still feels drawn to ending it all.

Scared and Confused

My life is so hard
I can't carry on.
It's too much to bear,
When I'm on my own.

I'm in a room full of people,
But I'm still on my own.
I feel like crying,
In this world all alone.

I'm on the outside looking in,
I am and feel like an outsider.
That's what they've done to me,
And I hate them for doing that.

My head takes control,
I want to be free,
And if that means dying,
Then let it be.

In this, the third poem, Jo recognises the value of being with others: 'it's too much to bear when I'm on my own.' But mixing with other people is a highly ambivalent business: she feels alone within the group, the outsider looking in; there is the feeling that others as well as herself make her an outsider. Freedom from depression is still associated with death, though the last verse (thankfully) lacks the harsh desperation of the earlier work.

Desperation

I feel so alone and so afraid,
And I don't know what to do,
Something's happening to me,
Something I can't control.

People are desperately trying to help,
And I can't understand why,
Because I don't and can't trust anyone,
I'm not used to people being on my side.

I keep writing and drawing things that are scary,
I've never felt so bad,
I don't really know how to explain it,
Oh God please help me.

I don't deserve to be alive or happy,
Everyone around me is happy and I'm not,
There's no light at the end of my tunnel,
And I can't find my way.

In the fourth poem, we see the beginning of a resolution of the ambivalence she feels in her association with other people. She is still alone, still afraid; but her fear is less associated with isolation and depression than with uncertainty about why she is starting to feel differently about her situation (verse 1). One is reminded of the proverb 'better the devil you know...'. When one is overwhelmed with insoluble problems or serious emotional pain, there is at least a sort of stability in the situation: one knows where one is. But change, even for the better, is unsettling. Jo finds that other people, surprisingly, are really trying to help her, and they cannot therefore be dismissed so easily as in the past. Her writings and drawings are described as scary – somewhat like the reference to the devil in the second poem: he is becoming more externalised. As Jo herself wonders, can she risk change, can she risk the possibility of being happier?

Finally, we have included the following jubilant poem written this year and associated with Jo's pregnancy. It is a celebration not only of the impending birth but also of her having found the capacity to love and be loved. She has found freedom in this, rather than in death and tears.

My Light, My New Beginning

I'm having a baby,
Can't you see,
Just how much
This means to me.

All the joys of being a mum,
All of it even the big bum.
I'm so happy can't you see,
Just how much it means to me.

For once in my life I'm happy
Like I've never been before.
The lights at the end of the tunnel,
And FINALLY I can see it.

I never thought I'd get to here,
I thought I'd always be stuck,
In that never ending nightmare,
But I'm NOT I'm FREE.

Profile of Amanda

Amanda is 20 years old and currently lives in bed and breakfast accommodation. She started writing only a year ago; all her poems and stories are typed and are presented beautifully in folders. She has four books:

1. Poems book

2. Feelings book

3. Shit book

4. Stuff book.

Amanda has lived with adoptive parents since the age of seven. Her natural parents live in a nearby city; she sees her mum but has no contact with her dad. She has returned home on a visit 'but it did not work out because I cause too much fighting. I hit people when they won't shut up.' She has three sisters, all older than herself, but she only has time for one of them. Amanda has written about the death of her niece (see below) and blames her sister for covering up the fact that her partner killed the eight-week-old baby.

Amanda sees a counsellor twice a week and a community psychiatric nurse every week. She does not like psychiatrists: 'They ask you to do stupid pictures.' She is proud of the fact that she has stopped taking anti-depressants on her own initiative. She has previously taken overdoses.

Amanda has written many poems, and has destroyed many which are no longer relevant to her feelings: as she would say, she has moved on. Those she keeps are carefully typed and filed, and these four poems are among those that she has selected for us as representing her most important work.

Alone

I'm alone again
Nothing to do
Listening to music
Boom, boom, boom.
My heart is broken up in two
I'm scared of dying
Really I am.
I talk to Scruffy and tell him
Who I am.
I'm a person
With a messed up head
Who really wanted to end up dead.
But, when I thought about how daft I'd been
I knew there was more to life I haven't seen.
I've often had enough of life,
Most of it I've hardly liked.
I can never talk about my feelings
But they really do need relieving.

Life

I've often had enough of life,
I often thought that it can't go on
Then, I thought that that was wrong.

I've been through hard times
Quite a bit in my life
Which has really given me a fright.

I felt that no one was ever there
Then I saw people really care
I can't express the way I feel
As I will only scream.

My parents were never nice to me
Even though I was innocent as can be
I was only a child when things went wrong,
I thought what on earth was going on
But when I got older
I found out stuff
That would make me go off in a huff
I know it was childish as can be,
But I couldn't think that that was me.

Then a couple of years ago
It came to me as a blow.
I remembered things my dad did to me
Even though I was meant to be free
Children don't know when things are wrong
But my parents knew what was going on.
My parents are the ones to blame
They're the ones who should have shame.

My adoptive parents are canny to me
I was thinking what can they see
I was horrible to them as can be
But they always forgive me.

Help Me

It seemed like my life was not worth living
Then I knew my brain was kidding
People are really canny to me
So why on earth can't I be!

What do other people see in me

There's the things that are bugging me

If I can see what they see in me
Maybe I'd be a bit free

I need to be free
Really I do

Free from the hurt
That some can't see.

I express my feelings by writing these
So please
Someone help me please

I need the stuff out of my head
That's really wanting me to end up dead.

Why? Why? Why?

Why am I feeling the way I feel?
Why do things happen?
Why do I hear things when no-ones around?
Why do I see things when others don't?
Why do I say things without thinking first?
Why do I feel so angry?
Why can't I see that people are just trying to help me?
Will someone be able to tell me before it's too late?

One is immediately struck by three characteristics of Amanda's work. First, her presentation is remarkably neat, and she types her poems so that they form patterns. Second, some poems (e.g. 'Life') present a serial personal history, rather than a snapshot of present emotions. (In this respect, they run in parallel to her stories – real and imaginary – which appear elsewhere in this book.) Third, Amanda makes occasional use of rhyming.

Thus, one can assume that, for Amanda, creating a schematic pattern – whether in recording one's life, or in the acts of writing and rhyming – is a useful way of making sense of past events and, potentially at least, of thinking about the future.

Clearly Amanda *works* at her poems: the ideas may be spontaneous, but are then crafted – essentially for her own satisfaction, rather than for sharing or impressing others. There are references to loneliness and sadness, to difficulties of communicating and even to a fear of dying. But one senses from the organisation and presentation of her thoughts that despair is not intense or insoluble. Her appreciation of her foster-parents is manifest, at least to herself and us, if not perhaps to them.

As in Jo's poems, there are references to ambivalent or ambiguous feelings about other people, to the need to achieve freedom, and to the need for help despite the difficulty of accepting its sincerity. Thus, Amanda appropriately ends this selection of her work with a wide range of questions. It would be impertinent (even plain stupid) for us to expect clarity in the answers, or even to hear her answers: there are few people more maddening than those who ask 'why?' about other people's feelings. But Amanda has achieved the ability to ask the right questions; and this is a good start.

Profile of Thomas

Thomas is 29 years old and has Tourette Syndrome. This was not diagnosed until he was 21. Until then it was generally thought that Thomas 'was doing things to get attention'. He has the compulsion to say things under his breath. He currently lives in a shared house; in the past he has lived in various hostels.

Thomas started writing when he was 15 years old. At the time he was 'trying to make songs up but left it to write poems'. At the time he was in a residential school and came home at weekends. Thomas had entered a poetry competition at school, which he won and then he started winning quite regularly. 'I was not good at explaining how I felt. It's a way of expressing my feelings.' He stayed at school until he was 17 years old and then went to an independent training unit.

Thomas does not work at present and is in receipt of benefit because of his disability. He acknowledges that there are some things he could not do, but 'I want to do something with my life.' He has always had the ambition to work for the Royal Mail. The hours would suit him as he would like to have the afternoons to himself. However, Thomas's lack of self-esteem and self-confidence is keeping him from applying for jobs at present.

Thomas is supported by a worker from the local community mental health team and sees a community psychiatric nurse every fortnight.

Thomas was never a fully integrated member of the writers' group at the Reach Out Project but he was in close touch with one of the workers, Caroline. He started using the project in 1997 and left four years ago just before his twenty-fifth birthday which is the age limit for the project.

A Little Understanding

Treat us like humans
I know that you can
with a little understanding.
You really care
about how we feel
and NOT forcing drugs
down us with our meal.
Talk to us, Treat us nice
and GIVE us helpful advice.
Don't say you understand
when you don't.
We won't co-operate
NO we won't.
Please don't ignore us
when we talk
or else we will walk.
So listen to us
Give us a chance
Just for once.

You Are...

You are not yourself
With a mental health
Because of all the drugs
They prescribe.
They tell you it'll make you better
But it doesn't – they just lie.
They think they know it all
And they treat you small.
They're patronising,
they think it's not surprising
because you're in care.
They don't listen
your voice isn't heard
so you have to
repeat it word for word.
Understanding not at all
they don't even call
you by your first name.
They treat you just like a patient
Not as a friend
But that's all I can say
So I'll have to end.

Thomas has received psychiatric treatment as inpatient and outpatient, and in these poems he sets out his experiences of professional help. No interpretation is necessary; they speak for themselves and sound their own warnings. Thomas's physical condition sometimes affects the way he walks, and he is conscious of people looking at him in the street.

Feet

Can you keep a secret?
Can you be discreet?
Can you understand
Without looking at my feet?
Avoiding looking at my face
Because I'm from a different place
And I suffer from mental health
Or anything else.

You don't like your life

You're in distress
And people think
You're a fucking pest.

You get angry
the way they treat you
as they still
look at your feet.
But you don't
let it
even though you
feel like shit.

But it's just the way
the world is
day after day.

As he has mentioned in 'You are…' he has been in care and now lives – somewhat precariously – in lodgings. The bleakness of this life, significantly expressed in capital letters, is set out in the following poem:

PLEASE LISTEN TO ME

IN YOUR MIND THERE'S NO ESCAPE
OF FEELING LOVE, FEELING HATE
FEELING LOW SOMETIMES
AND THEN YOU FEEL FINE
FEELING PEOPLE'S LET YOU DOWN
ON YOUR FACE YOU'VE GOT A FROWN
NEEDING SOMEONE TO PICK YOU UP
WHEN YOU FEEL LIKE SHIT
NEEDING TO SPEAK TO SOMEONE WHO CARES
BUT THEY'RE NOT ALWAYS THERE
WHEN YOU NEED EM
THEY LET YOU DOWN
MOST OF THE TIME THEY ONLY CARE
WHEN YOU'VE DONE A CRIME
THEN THEY WANT TO SPEAK TO YOU
OUT OF THE BLUE
I'VE TOLD YOU I'VE BEEN THERE
ALL BEFORE
AND I CAN'T STAND IT ANYMORE
BUT JUST LISTEN.

In the following poems, Thomas reflects on the suffering caused by his father – the memory of which never loses its power – and on what he would like to say to his mother. Sadly, despite the tenderness of this latter poem (or perhaps because of it), he has never steeled himself to send his mother a copy.

Can't Close My Eyes

I can't close my eyes
As when I do
I see the past I don't like
It gets worse at night
When you're on your own
In your bedroom alone
I don't feel like fun
When I think about what I've done
I see my dad bullying me
If only he could see
What I'm going through now
but how?
Could I tell him
That I get upset
Even when I close my eyes
And think about what he's done
To his own son.

Dear Mum

Dear mum I wrote you this letter
Hoping that things will get better
I do feel lonely without you here
And I love you is what I'd like to hear
I know the times we've had
Have been good and bad
And there's times when we've fell out
But that's what arguments are all about
All those times I've made you worry
But I really am sorry
I love you mum you're my friend
And all that love I have to send
I don't want it back

And I want you to keep it forever
And all those dreams
For ever and ever.

Thomas's main support and security has come from the Reach Out Project, to which he has written this poem:

Young Hearts

We learn to be happy
We learn not to be sad
We learn to talk about
What drives us mad.
We talk about how we feel
Emotions we show are real
We talk with our hearts
on our sleeves
and what kind of help we need.
When we finish we feel a bit better
It's better than writing a letter.

Profile of Steven

Steven is a 23-year-old skilled mathematician. He has experienced significant mental health problems and drug dependency issues. He could not be interviewed face to face because he was hospitalised on a Section and was not due any leave. He agreed to be interviewed by telephone. He said, 'I'm not really a poetry man.' He has only written the one poem and that was when he was going to a conference to help with a presentation by the Reach Out Project nearly three years ago.

When we were collecting material for this book, Steven agreed to the inclusion of this poem.

What is 'ove

'ove is 'eaven
'ove is L
Love is the happy medium
'ove is from the heart
Love can be made from art
'ove you can't buy
'ove is high
Love is why
How is 'ove
When is 'ove
Love probably is the happy medium

Steven commented that he was not into poetry: he prefers painting, and has designed the presentation of the Reach Out newsletters and earlier collections of writings. We wanted, however, to include this poem: like Amanda's work, it presents a visual design to enhance its meaning – the fragmentation of thought is doubly expressed. Furthermore, it is wryly amusing and open to various interpretations. (Unfortunately we were unable to check out with Steven the circumstances of his writing.)

Elsewhere in this book, there is a presentation from a children's group (Chapter 9) where the focus of work is reliance on metaphor – where meaning is implicit rather than overt. Steven's poem suggests an adult equivalence. The flow of ideas has broken down. Love has lost its head, and is perhaps in hospital with Steven. What is missing is L: perhaps love is hell. Love lies somewhere between sense and madness. Perhaps this happy medium cannot be achieved. Perhaps it is wholly elusive (or illusory) as it alternates between honesty and the artificiality of an art form.

Profile of Gemma

Gemma is 18 years old and currently lives in supported lodgings, which she hates. She has been there for over a year and is hoping to move out soon. She was sexually abused as a child by a family friend. The case did not go to court as it would have been her word against his.

She likes to write and found it helpful to put some of her feelings on paper. Gemma has always liked writing stories from a very early age. She has lost the diaries she wrote when she was young. Between 11 and 13 she began writing more; and also again at 15. She does not write at all now. She did want to write a book about what had happened to her and a journalist at a local newspaper was interested in getting it published but she 'became scared' and backed out. 'I started thinking "What would people think?" I'm so young. I also wanted it to be private.'

Now she works with children who have been through similar problems and would like to go to university to become a social worker or children's nurse.

In the following poems, selected by Gemma, she records her feelings over a period of about three years, during which she moved from membership of a writing group to volunteer helper in a children's therapeutic group.

Gemma has added her own comments on the sense behind each poem.

My Mask

I wear a mask visible to only my mind –
to hide my personality's blemishes,
I need one to hide behind.

You may think I'm confident and happy,
don't believe me because I'm not.
The truth is that underneath
I really hurt a lot.

I'm not superhuman, I too can feel pain.
Remember that in future,
before hurting my feelings again.

My mask is my only protection
from your vicious taunts,
And if I try to take it off,
they come back to haunt.

One day I may remove it
and show you the real me,
only if you'll accept me as I am
and finally let me be.

Author's comments

'My Mask' is about having a 'secret side' that people don't know about or under-stand.

To Be Free

My hair blows free behind me
as I grasp the horse's mane.
Us and the river side by side
no looking back from where we came.

The Sun rises ahead of us
casting golden shadows everywhere.
The beauty of the land
is here for us to share.

Galloping free and easy
across the grass and flowers,
sending petals in the air
which float around us in a shower.

Hooves pound the ground,
wind blows in my face.
Cool air fills my lungs,
this moment I embrace.

For nothing is better
than to roam the country free.
Lost in its beauty,
the only place to be.

The company of the animals
the sky and the trees,
everything ahead of us
is there for us to see.

The two best things in life
are freedom and nature.
Freedom to live our lives
and at peace with every creature.

Author's comments

'To Be Free' was written at a difficult time when I wanted to escape.

In Her Eyes

Her eyes held the truth of fear and pain,
years of tears shed again and again.

Her smile was bright,
her eyes were sad.
Her face was a shield
of dark memories she had.

Full of emotion, piercing and deep,
her eyes sparkled, but only to weep.

Her face was deceiving,
her eyes were clear.
Her face was for you,
her eyes were for her.

Your eyes hold the truth of what lies in your soul,
look in their eyes –
they carry all that's untold.

Author's comments

*'In Her Eyes' is also about having a 'secret side' that people don't know about but
also about putting on a front when underneath all I wanted was for someone to
notice that I needed someone.*

Clear Out

I'm casting aside my sadness,
pouring away my pain.
Filling myself with strength
to flow out from within.

Bad times packed in little boxes
with the lid firmly closed.
Space just to look forward
to the good times I will know.

I'll lock my fears in a cage,
have the key thrown away.
Close the door to terror
and welcome every day.

I won't take my anger with me,
I'll leave my hatred too.
Revenge will be my success
in anything that I do.

Regrets burned on an open fire,
guilt rising up as smoke.
I'll believe I did the best
that circumstance could provoke.

I won't take anything with me.
Just my will to go on.
Faith that things will get better
this hope I've had all along.

I will walk out of the darkness,
Then close the door behind.
Open my eyes to the light,
finally have peace of mind.

Author's comments

After a very long break of rarely writing anything I wrote 'Clear Out'. This is the most recent and shows how I feel, even though it's difficult, that it's time to put my experiences behind me and move on.

The poems were not written with the same outburst of spontaneity as is found among the other young writers. For Gemma, orderliness of presentation arises from a great deal of reflective thought which both clarifies her feelings while reducing their overt negativity – though not their impact on the reader. The final poem shows considerable personal courage, a good level of poetic competence and the achievement, with the help she has received, of personal integrity.

Profile of Alex

Alex is 17 years old. She currently lives on her own in a flat; she had been there for seven months at the time of interview. She came into residential care at the age of eight because she had been sexually abused; she was abused again when she was in care.

Alex started writing when she was ten years old when she was seeing a counsellor, who encouraged her to write. Her writing is dependent on her mood. Sometimes she can sit and write for hours and writes 'loads'. She used to write in her bedroom when she was in care, but now writes in the sitting room of her flat. Previously she has handwritten her work, but she sometimes types now because of arthritis in her fingers. She has 'binned' a lot of her work, but workers at the Open Door Project kept a lot of what she was going to throw out. Alex likes to read 'War poetry': 'I read it over and over again.' She also likes Roald Dahl books. Her ambition is to work for the NSPCC.

Alex started writing with the encouragement of members of a writing group for sexually abused children. Since then she has written 22 poems, from which she has made the following selection. The first poem was written at the age of ten, and is remarkable work for a young child.

Nobody!

For each day that comes,
The sun goes down,
For each night that comes,
I'm rapped tight in fright,
Hoping that I have the
Strength in mind to get rid
Of the pain of being a nobody.

When each time I'm sick with
Trying to find the answers,
And crying when trying to find
The courage to stop being a
Nobody.

When I put on my disguise,
And swear I will win somehow,
The gaze of life comes looking
For me disguised by those around,
And the pain gets worse of being
A nobody.

When I hope to stop the fearful
Shadows of worry from getting
Too near,
The singing of shame begins to
Get louder,
And as my eyes fill with water,
I begin

Certain themes are apparent, all arising from the abuse she had suffered two years previously: continuing fright when she goes to bed (though by this time she was in residential care), the sense of not being a real person, the shame, the crying – whether from pain or from guilt. The extent to which these feelings persist and may even harden into permanence is illustrated by the following two short and bitter poems.

Sex is Punishment

Sex is bad
Sex is sad
Sex is non stop talk 4 lads

Sex is crap
Sex will be scrapped
Sex is one big trap

Sex makes you sore
Sex makes you throw
Sex makes you a whore

A Note to my Guilt

Why do you come to me
Why not the fucking criminals
Why do you follow me with your friend fear
Why do you make me cry so many tears.

Please tell me what makes me bad
What makes you get so mad
Leave me alone, I need to be on my own.

In the latter poem, Alex resents how she, the victim, feels guilt, rather than the perpetrator who assaulted her. She is nagged by guilt as a secondary inner self, similar to Jo's experience of the inner devil. The crying and fear have continued even eight years after the abuse took place.

There is also some hardening of resentment against her parents who have, in her eyes, abandoned her to residential care and, recently, to an independent and lonely local authority tenancy.

My Letter Home

If I was to send a letter home
I wouldn't know where to begin
Would I send it to my mum
Would I send it to my dad.

If I was to send a letter home
It wouldn't change the way they think
It wouldn't make them change a bit
It wouldn't put them where they belong
Though they know that they were wrong.

If I was to send a letter home
I would have no answers
They would still be able to hurt
They would still be able to live.

If I was to send a letter home
What would I share?
How much could I bear?
I couldn't even give them a glare.

If I was to send a letter home
What would it say apart from why?
Would it say I HATE you or
You will pay?

Alex has recently written two poems which directly and powerfully describe what an eight-year-old girl feels after forced sexual intercourse with her father. The first, which is Alex's own favourite poem, is written with a bitter whimsicality of style, like a horrific nursery rhyme. The second is more muted, and is the group facilitator's favourite. It comes closest of all Alex's work to the Wordsworthian view of poetry as emotion recollected in tranquillity. But the tranquillity is more apparent than real, and the message is timeless: a powerful memorial to spoiled innocence.

Devil

There was a little girl
Thought she saw the devil
Though she didn't understand
What was going to happen.

Fear all around
Even on the ground
People shouting real loud
There was such a crowd.

There was a little girl
Thought she saw the devil
Left torn apart, sad and all alone
What did she do so bad?

Fell asleep, but woke up
Thought it was a dream
That could not be real.

There was a little girl
Thought she saw the devil
Curled up in the corner, only to find
The worst thing on her mind.

Photo on the floor
Should have ran out the door
Still she didn't understand
What the fuck just happened

Powerless

No voice, no choice
Tired and all cried out
Angry yet ashamed
Helpless and vulnerable
It was me that they blamed.

No voice, no choice
Scared and quiet
Sore and unsure of what just happened
It was me that they blamed.

No voice, no choice
Shocked and confused
Hungry and feeling so dirty
It was me that they blamed.

CHAPTER 6

Using Poetry 2: Poems Presented by the Other Adults

Again, the following poems have been selected by their authors, and are presented in the same format as for Chapter 5.

Profile of Beccy

Beccy is 26 years old and currently studying for a Diploma in Social Work. She was 'sexually abused by three different people…two family members and a foster parent'. The abuse started when she was four years old; she was taken into care when she was 14 and remembers this as a very bad experience. After being abused in the foster home she went into a children's home where she stayed for three and a half years. This was a very positive experience for her. Beccy says she loved school 'because when I was there I wasn't at home'. She went to college to do her A levels and then did an Access course before starting the Diploma in Social Work.

Beccy started writing when she was 14 years old. A friend started writing to her and Beccy wrote back. She has self-harmed in the past, overdosed several times and made one serious attempt at suicide when she was 19.

Beccy was one of the writers who responded to our advertisement; she says she thought long and hard before submitting three poems which she said were essentially suicide notes. Beccy has

---

always kept her poems in a file which she calls 'Eternity': 'I've changed the folder over the years but I've always put a sticker on the front with this name on it. I originally called the file "Eternity" because it's what it felt like to me: eternity where there was no end to it.'

Beccy has never written a journal as such but she has started to write her 'life story': 'I started writing this when I decided to make a success of my life, when I was 22. I've only gotten to the part when I went into care because I only write about four times a year. After I'm qualified I plan to get it published some day, that's my dream anyway.'

What follows are some of Beccy's poems. A point she made clearly in interview is that it is important to be able to accept one's own feelings: 'Sometimes your feelings can shock you. Sometimes when I was writing I felt that I hated people, but what I wrote about was loving those people. It was difficult to acknowledge that deep down I loved the people who abused me. It needs to be pointed out that people can have a wide range of feelings towards the people who've hurt them, and they won't always be negative.'

Beccy is now married, and has made a remarkable self-adjustment when one thinks of the longstanding sexual abuse – multiple abuse at that – which she suffered from a very early age. As we would expect, she (like Gemma and like Alex's final poem) now writes calmly and thoughtfully, though the ambivalence particularly towards her father is still strong.

She has written powerfully about the problems of forgiveness and reconciliation, the achievement of which is essential to her own maturity and integrity.

Dad There's Things You Should Know

You were my life, my light, my world,
I was always your precious little girl.
You loved me so much, but in a cruel way,
You still don't know what you did wrong, not even to this day.

I know you loved me.
I suppose you always did,

But please Dad realise I was only a kid.
You got mixed up with the type of love you should give,
And now I'm torn apart because of what you did.

I love you so much,
But you'll never know,
Because we have to part,
One of us has to go.

I hope one day you will forgive me for what I will do,
But please believe me I have no choice, it's all because of you.

Don't get me wrong, I'm not perfect in any way,
But it hurts when you tell me you did nothing wrong,
You still say that to my face, even today.

You thought we were special,
Because of what we had.
But I was your daughter and you were my Dad.

The love you gave me was wrong from the start, It's meant for two
adults, it comes from the heart.
You followed your heart,
In which sense couldn't entail,
You've destined me to turmoil on an endless trail.

You gave me love of husband and wife,
It only brought us strife.
You couldn't love me as daughter and Dad,
And now we are both terribly sad.

I'll never know everything,
I hope I never do,
But Dad I know this, I love you.
Dad believe me because it's true,
I love you, I love you,
But not the things you do.
Why did you do it?
I suppose I'll never know.
You can't admit you did wrong,
So you have to go.

We can't stay together, and we can't stay apart,
Why couldn't you follow morality, and not your heart?
Did you know that what you were doing was wrong?
I was a child and you an adult,
So it was wrong.

All I can say is that I love you very much.
In time I will forgive you, but I'm not ready yet.
Time heals but we must never meet again,
Because the heartache I would feel,
Would bring me to an end.

Beccy wrote this at the age of 19, and in discussion was able – as recorded in the profile – to define the nature of the ambivalence she felt. She went on to comment that most people assume that hatred towards the aggressor is the normal and only possible response. Yet victims may experience a wide range of feelings towards those who have hurt them: 'It's quite natural to have some positive feelings towards those people, especially if not all of the relationship has been abusive.'

This very reasonable approach is not, however, without the potential for further suffering, partly because ambivalence – the presence of mixed and contradictory feelings – is very complex. Sometimes moral considerations seem to require a more positive attitude than one honestly feels; and in such a situation what happens to the carefully controlled and unexpressed negative attitudes? Two years after the earlier poem, Beccy wrote:

Gone

What will happen when I die?
Will anyone want to cry?
At my funeral I will be,
One of two people,
The priest and me,
An empty church with no-one there,
No-one there because no-one cares,
No-one will notice I have gone,
Everyone thinking I have done wrong,
'B' matters to only the dead,
Her lonely heart is never fed,
How can she live when people hate?
Hate her breathing, the hatred so great,
She stands at the coffin and looks at her face,
A face so young, but the heartache great,
She was there to torture and hurt,
She blamed herself, she thought she was a flirt,

She was there to be a punchbag,
It didn't matter that it made her sad,
Everything she had was taken away,
Her innocence, her youth, her dreams,
Not one of them allowed to stay,
She longed to be happy so very much,
She needed to be loved so very much,
She was on her own, and she knew it well,
No-one could enter her personal hell,
She wanted a hand to guide her through,
She needed a hug,
And a voice saying, 'I love you'.

Here we can see the welling-up of negativism which had apparently been so reasonably dealt with earlier. There is a reiteration of hatred, but directed against herself. We observe her as she looks at herself in the coffin. Beccy has commented that she wrote this shortly after the suicide of a close friend when she too felt like killing herself. Writing this painful poem proved to be a lifeline: she realised that her friend's death had been pointless and that her own death would not really matter to those to whom, morally, it should matter. The poem achieves a wistful longing for affection, but within a harsh fatalistic kind of stoicism.

How reliable are social workers and other carers in recognising this complex response? Beccy has written:

Barriers

You are the vision of a future me,
Of what I know, I could be,
I want to be like you,
But I don't know if I can do it too.

I take one step forward,
And two back,
Because of what happened in my past.

I can do it in my heart,
But in my mind, it falls apart.

I want to be where you are,
But I have to work twice as hard,
Then my dream seems too far.

I want to see you as a friend,
Someone who a hand will lend.
I want us to be equal,
But social workers come in sequel.

Even if you can be a friend,
Our relationship has to end.
You can't be a friend for life,
And that adds to the monotonous strife.

It's hard to keep people,
Then someone else joins the sequel.
No-one sticks around long enough,
And that makes my life really tough.
No-one sees how I turned out,
That makes me want to hit out.

In my heart I know you care,
But only while you have to be there,
After that I do not know,
Because rules say you have to go.

In my heart I want you there,
All I want is someone to care,
As much as I want you as a friend,
When your job is done,
Your hand you can not lend.
Because of this we are on different sides,
And I don't think that is very kind.

Why do I have to keep losing people?
Why is there always a sequel?
I know people have to move on,
But why don't they care when their job is done?

They all say they'll keep in touch,
But they never do,
And that hurts so much.

I often wonder if they think of me,
While having a biscuit and a cup of tea,
But there's a lot of things they're blind to see,
They always miss the real me.

Bubbles

I live in a world I'm not part of,
There's a barrier between us,
A thick dense fog,
It's like walking around in a bubble of air,
People on the outside don't have a care,
Trapped in a world that only I know,
Life going by at a rate of snail-slow,
Where ever I am I feel distant and apart,
Locked outside of my real life,
By the agony in my heart,
The only comfort is someone the same as me,
A person held back from life by secrecy,
We walk around in bubbles of air,
Knowing that people don't really care,
We're locked out of the world at large,
Made to live by ourselves where life is hard,
But even then I'm still on my own,
I'm still left feeling all alone,
For all we are both locked out of life,
We both have to cope with personal strife,
Our bubbles can touch but never join,
The same experiences but by different loins,
Different people but same experience you see,
Others cannot feel what I feel,
That's restricted to only me.

There is a continuing sadness and loneliness here, a feeling that isolation is modified only by the nearness of others in similar plights. But even then, the bubbles remain personal and separate; understanding can never be *wholly* shared.

Beccy has solved virtually all the problems associated with early sexual abuse: she has moved further than Jo, for example, and has had more years to achieve this kind of movement. But she and Jo have at least one thought in common: for Jo, time had stood still and was tantamount to a prison; Beccy's poems (as she has already told us) are kept in a file labelled 'Eternity' – there are times when for Beccy also, time stands still. Here are two final poems from her on how far change is *really* possible, and what she has *really* hoped for.

Always Trying

The world spins 'round and 'round,
My heart goes up and down,
Life is so hard,
I feel that I will drown.

Even if I make it,
To even get the dream,
My heart on the inside,
Will never be as it seems.

Made into something,
I don't want to be,
Changed into something,
That wasn't meant to be.

Born as one thing,
Changed into another,
Can't go back to the born thing,
Have to stay as the other.

You can't change what was done,
Nothing can take it away,
Even if I have a good life,
It will be there every day.

Guardian Angel

Take my hand and hold it tight,
Be my eyes when tears blind my sight,
Use your ears when everyone else is deaf,
Be there for me when everyone else has left,
Run with me across the hills,
Be my freedom when I'm imprisoned by evil and ill-will,
Break the chains that hold me down,
Be my smile when my face frowns,
Fly with me through the breeze,
Be my courage and strength to leave,
Hug me so I know someone cares,
Be my shadow so someone's there.

Profile of Indie Larma

Indie Larma is 32 years old and at the time of interview was working in a residential school for emotionally disturbed boys. She was abused physically and emotionally by her father, who was an alcoholic. She is one of a set of triplets and her mother and sisters were also beaten by her father, who left when the girls were eight years old.

Indie Larma has a clear memory of the day her father left. Neighbours came round, having heard noise during the night before. When they were told what had happened, Indie Larma saw 'the horror in their faces' but what has stayed with her is that 'They were enjoying what I was saying and wanted to hear more. I made the conscious decision that I was never going to talk about it again.' Her mother and sisters did not talk about the abuse at that time; her mother can now discuss it with Indie Larma but not with her sisters. She says her mother 'talks about things about which I have no recollection'.

Indie Larma describes herself as being 'delinquent and attention-seeking' when at school, but at the same time 'I was shy and quiet'. Her mother and stepfather persuaded her to go into the army when she was 19 years old. She believes this was the making of her because it 'unleashed the tiger'. She remained in the army for four years. Indie Larma 'fell into the job' at the residential school. She had applied for the part-time post of child care officer and then went full-time; she remained there for seven years. She is currently studying for a degree in psychology with the Open University and is torn between whether to go down the social work or psychology career path in the future: 'My guide in life is to help people have fun.'

Indie Larma started writing poetry when she was seeing a counsellor, who had suggested she try to express what she was feeling through writing. The poems below are a selection from those she wrote in the past but they also include how she felt after being interviewed.

In the poems of Jo and Gemma, we have seen how writing is sometimes associated with the sensation of a second self in conflict with the 'real' self. The ideas of a real self and of unalloyed feelings are overridden by ambiguities and mixed (ambivalent) emotions, in respect both of the abusive aggressor and of one's own integrity – one's sense of wholeness and personal worth.

In interview, Indie Larma was able to express this complexity with considerable clarity: sometimes, having written a poem, she would return to it and think, 'Blimey, did I really do that? It was as if there were two different people.' And sometimes, after writing a poem, she felt that a massive weight had been lifted from her shoulders and (paradoxically) would cry for long periods.

The sense of two people is conveyed in several of her poems. In the following, she is both miserable and resilient and – in parallel with this – those who care about her are both resented and appreciated (verses 4 and 6).

Don't Drown the Clown

Feelin miserable today
But I don't know why
Want to tuck myself away
From the world and cry.

Some people out to get me
They say they're my mates and care
So why given the chance
My skin they would tear.

But try keeping a happy dog down
A fun lovin clown
Who's not gonna drown
Especially a sound person like me.

You took me on, built me up
Aspirations, the whole damn lot
All changed now, threat that I pose
But you don't understand.

Try keeping me down, the clown
Who's not gonna drown
The clown who's gonna keep you afloat
And not sink your boat.

The moral of the song,
Is don't shit on those that care

Just because they speak their minds
And say things that others don't dare.

Don't Drown the Clown…

From her writings over several years, Indie Larma was asked to select the
poem which had most meaning for her. It represents an important stage in
coming to terms with the abuse suffered by herself, her sisters and her
mother: it was the turning point between dwelling in the past and moving
on to future emotional freedom. It was written in the train following a
visit home, in which she had confronted her mother with the facts of her
abuse, and her mother had been honest in return. Indie Larma felt that, to
some extent, the air had been cleared and that relationships could be
more honest than in the past. Understandably, a showdown of this
importance leaves a residual need for a more personal catharsis, and Indie
Larma wrote:

Home

I've gone home
Not knowing what I'd find
Yes I went blinkered
But this time not blind

I'm holding a trophy
About the knowledge I've gained
So why do I feel
So horribly pained

I'm crying salty tears
Deep retching inside
I'm on the train
So the tears I hide

Horrors of thunder
And of the dark
Howlett has really
Made his mark

Arms up knickers down
Spend loadsa money
Your sorrows
Will drown

Hanging, woods,
Shot with a gun
You fuckin little bastards
What have you done?

I'm gonna make you suffer
You've ruined my life
I beat for that
My lovin wife.

Rejection is a thing
We all three fear
By dealing with this
We will pull near.

Pictures and poems
Talking things through
Moving me on
To green pastures anew.

The anger and frustration remain, as shown in verses 5, 6 and 7, and it will take more time for these to be resolved. A beginning is shown in the final verses. As the next poem recognises, the rubble of past disappointments cannot ever be cleared away; but it can be used as a foundation for building a new life and new hopes.

Love

Love is not a game
Where the board can be wiped clean.

Love is not a game
Where the pieces can be seen.

Love is one wrong move
And another brick in place.

Love is bashing down defences
But not clearing the debris away.

Love is building on rubble
And flowers growing up the wall.

Love is…

This selection of Indie Larma's work ends with an emphatic statement, in which the underlining is essential to its intrinsic meaning. 'People need love and affection: if you can't feel that, you are in a lost world.' As she herself commented in discussion, the key issue is how far to enter new situations in which one risks suffering further, though different, kinds of abuse, and how far the memories of past events should be allowed to colour the future. This statement was written at a time of recurrent nightmares; these cannot be controlled, but should not impede recognition of the possibility of future hope and contentment.

Stumbling

Love and affection is a basic need
Without these I have no feet

So where I am stumbling, nobody knows
Where I am stumbling, nobody goes

Vague ideas about me and my past
Feelings and dreams consciously felt

The sweats, the panting, the shouting out loud
I need to be comforted, I need to be held

And so I am now, feeling safe and encompassed
Enveloped in swirling mists of time – suspended…

Profile of Laura

Laura is 46 years old and is a tutor assessor in the care sector. She was sexually abused between the ages of two and ten by her father and his friends. She first disclosed this just before she was 40. A lot of memories had been repressed. She used to work with older people and unexpectedly found herself working with a paedophile, which opened up many painful memories: this was the reason she disclosed her earlier experiences to her supervisor. At that time she was working for a social services department, which arranged for her to see a specialist counsellor; and she also attended a group which used transactional analysis.

Laura left home when she was 16 and has no contact with her father. It was only last year that she told her mother about the abuse. Her response was that Laura must have false memory syndrome and that it could never have happened because he did not even like Laura. Her father was a violent man who abused her mother but 'he only hit me once. It was more psychological abuse – the fear. It would have been better to be hit.'

'The sexual abuse started as "fun" with other children and playing while being filmed … later it was more serious "prostitution". But my father only ever sexually abused me to assert power or as a punishment – it was usually violent and silent, except for some explicit language telling me what I was! The rest of the time he would belittle me or ignore me, nothing was ever good enough – except in company when he showed off his clever little girl!'

Laura was sexually assaulted by her father and his friends over a period of eight years, and these assaults were accompanied not by expressions of affection but by ridicule and contempt. Her experience was therefore of multiple abuse which damaged her physically and emotionally, and destroyed her sense of self-worth.

With the help of a social worker, she began to express her feelings when she was about 40 years old and – because of difficulties in verbalising them – was encouraged to write them down. 'I wrote these when I was going through the process of recalling memories which so distressed me that I could hardly bear to talk about them.'

Laura's relationship with her mother was difficult: 'I had little recourse to mothering as my mother was often ill… My mother was always busy/ill/depressed and pushing me to achieve at school and I could never talk to her – I felt caught as I had to help my mum.'

Words

Words
Power
The words a child should never have to hear.
The words that crush her adoration of him.
The words that bring fear of the pain,
That oh so surely will follow.

The Words
The Power
The power that comes from imagination provoked.
The power that keeps the secret.
The power that tames her spirit
Till it's captured, imprisoned in time.

The words have the power to stay
When the speaker has long since gone.
They echo in the child who remains
And keep her where they say she belongs.

The child's been asleep for so long,
But something awakes her now.
She wants to tell of the secret
But the echoes are there and so loud.

But there's Words
But there's Power.
These are words that are kind and supporting,
These are words that reach out to the child.
These are words that say she is precious,
It's safe to speak out and be heard.

There's Words
There's Power
The power words give to the child,
The power that helps her be strong,
The power to challenge the words of the past,
To face them, do battle and win.

This poem clearly and helpfully emphasises the relationship between the use of words and the exercise of power; and it shows how these two concepts have, with help, been transferred from the degradation imposed by her father to the achievement of release from the past: she has finally won the battle.

Profile of Sue

Sue is 44 years old and responded to an advertisement to submit poetry for publication in this book. Sue was sexually abused by her father between the ages of 5 and 17. She miscarried her father's baby when she was 17. The abuse stopped when she married; she has now been married for 23 years. She has known her husband (who was emotionally abused as a child) since she was seven years old as they lived next door to each other: 'We came together when my parents fell apart.' They have two children: 'We made every effort to ensure the children were going to be safe.'

At the time of interview Sue was working for a local voluntary organisation and was involved in various activities with other victims of abuse, for example, running a helpline on the Internet for people who self-harm. Sue is training to become a counsellor and hopes to qualify in three years.

Soon after interview she was diagnosed as having bipolar disorder. Sue says the consultant psychiatrist 'was clear in his opinion that this was triggered by the severe and continual trauma experienced by me in my formative years… He seemed convinced that this, or any other sort of trauma, does have a direct impact on the long term mental health of people.'

Sue started writing in her early teenage years and then again in her twenties. 'It was a relief to write. The poems were directly for my benefit. I wrote what I wanted to say to my dad and couldn't.' Her mother was also physically and emotionally abused by her father, but 'she is in denial. He manipulated her. She saw and still sees him through rose tinted glasses.'

Sue's experiences of abuse and of degradation were similar to Indie Larma's. While the assaults continued, she found a teacher whom she trusted, and although unable to tell her about her problems, she wrote the following poem for her.

Please Miss?

Please Miss?
Can I stay with you?
Please Miss?
Look I've lost my shoe!
Please Miss?
Can I please stay today?
My Mom is always cryin'
Daddy's gone away.
Please Miss?
My arm is cut!
It was caught in the lock
As the door slammed shut!
Please Miss?
My leg is bleedin'
Right at the top
Where there is no feelin'.
Please Miss?
My Daddy's back
They wont't stop fightin'
Look my eye's all black!
Please Miss?
Will you hear my words?
I know I can't write
And I can't be heard
But Please Miss?
Just look into my eyes
Could a child of six
Really be this wise?

Please Miss???????

Unfortunately, the teacher suffered major illness and the poem was never given to her.

It is a useful example of how a serious and central problem may not be directly stated but may be implicit in the description of various symptomatic and tangential issues. In this instance, we read about the need for care away from home; the black eye; marital problems; self-harm (the cuts on her arm and leg are accompanied – or masked – by very unlikely excuses). One is reminded again of Steven's poem and of the children's group 'working through metaphor'.

This tangential approach to stating her problems persisted in later years; it is evident in the following poem, written when Sue's father was terminally ill and when she was therefore compelled to come to terms with the acute ambivalence she felt about him. The poem was also a reminder to others that 'what people were seeing was not what was going on inside' – i.e. both inside the family and within herself.

The Mask

There's a face behind the mask,
Hidden from view.
Dreams tell the secrets
Known only by few.
'She's always smiling'
The unknowing say.
But tears fall so often
Just under the skin.
She works many hours,
But knows not why.
Today she just sits,
You don't see her cry.
Tears fall in torrents,
Silently drop.
Memories abhorrent,
When will they stop?
She owns her own thoughts
Thoughts so intense.
Her love can't be bought
But passions incensed.
The child within
Is the person she seeks,
Hidden so deeply,
They may never meet.
'Can you see me?'
Please say 'NO'
Don't laugh as she passes,
Just let her go.

Sue has said about her father, 'I loved him dearly but hated the sight of him.' In the following poem, she expresses this by reviewing her childhood. She recalls the physical pain of sexual assault, hiding under the bedclothes, and the impossibility of telling her mother what was happening. The poem illustrates how abuse creates guilt in the child (as Alex also found). The reader is left with the realisation that, though her father's death is imminent and though she does not wish him to suffer pain, what he did to her will never be wholly resolved.

Of The Night

The light has faded
Daytime's gone
Night is here
My time has come.

Am I dreaming
Or is it real?
There is such pain
But I cannot feel.

I pull the covers
Please let me hide
Soon be over
It hurts inside.

Hush little baby
Don't say a word
No use trying
You can't be heard.

He says he loves me
Am I to blame?
Give in, it's easy
I feel such shame.

I'm so afraid
To be in his care
So young, and yet
Aware.

Is it love
Or maybe hate?
Ask God above
To keep me safe.

Father
I was in your care
Betrayed my trust
It is not fair.
Now a man
So weak, so sick
I love you Father
Let death be quick.

Profile of Vera

Vera is 67 years old and attended the first all-female group to be set up by Beyond Existing. Vera had previously been involved in a research project which was considering the needs of older women who had been abused.

Vera had been a victim of domestic violence throughout her marriage. She was a victim of physical, sexual, emotional, financial abuse and gross neglect. She was referred to the social work department after she was admitted to hospital having been starved by her husband; at the time of admission it was thought she would not survive. After recovering and with the help of a social worker and police domestic violence officer, Vera left her husband and subsequently divorced him. Her husband had always threatened to keep Vera pregnant; in fact she had ten pregnancies but only two sons survived, one of whom has learning disabilities.

Vera has always written poetry and kept a journal. In the Beyond Existing group she read poetry she had written in the past but also shared her recent writings – poetry and journal entries (see Chapter 7).

Vera is now in old age. Hers has been a harsh life: poverty, cruelty from her husband, regrets over an earlier lost love, the loss of children. Through the support of members of her group, she is now able to record in her journal and her poetry a kind of reconciliation with the past and her acceptance of a more peaceful ending.

Recovery

I want to live my life alone,
Do what I want all on my own.
Rid myself of hate and pain,
Live my life and be happy again.
Find laughter and joy each wakening day,
Be rid of the sadness that gets in my way.
The hurt I feel from dusk till dawn,
For those I lost and now do mourn.

Hurt that cut deep like a knife,
Has been the cause of a miserable life.
Times of want I know so well,
Living in a place of man made hell.
Tears I shed when feeling so sad,
I long to replace by feeling glad.
Doing things that me alone will please,
Be rid of the one who makes me ill at ease.

I want good health to add to my joy,
Or must I suffer the one who hurts and annoys.
Alone to give each day a smile,
Look out at the world for a long while.
The quiet as I sit on my own,
No plans to travel or to roam.
Visit friends who are quite near,
No feeling of sadness only cheer.

To be alone will cause no despair,
But will show me who really cares.
The sorrow and grief will not stay,
But swiftly lift and go away.
No sleepless nights no heartfelt woe,
As I have dreamt of the day you go.
So now my life will be lived to the full,
Complete and joyful the gentle lull.

Day by Day

In this journal I am living day to day,
Nothing much happens any way.
I have had my share of sorrow and pain,
And swear it will not happen again.

My disability rules my life in what I do,
As it controls me I will fight that is true.
If you know me you will not ask why,
To be on this earth I did almost die.

But now thanks to those who made me survive
Kind caring people who kept me alive.
Now I have a future be it long or short
True friends I made none were bought.
As the time passes the past fades away,
My journal gives me an outlet day by day.
I had good people like Jill* and Phil*,
Then Jacki* came into my life and is in it still.

[*Jill – social worker; Phil – domestic violence police officer; Jacki – group leader]

Past events cannot be forgotten or condoned, even after many years. It would be facile to say that Vera has 'come to terms' with the past. But she has certainly come to terms with herself, accepting who she is and forgiving what, in herself, may have contributed directly or indirectly to earlier harsh events and experiences. This is, perhaps, a significant element in what is meant by the phrase 'making a good end'.

Profile of Denise

Denise is 40 years old. She has been a victim of both child abuse and domestic violence. She started attending the third Beyond Existing group two years ago after she was referred by her community psychiatric nurse. Denise has a history of mental health problems and self-harm.

Denise was abused physically and sexually by her own father and then sexually abused by her stepfather, by whom she had three daughters. She also has a son from another relationship. Denise has also been a victim of domestic violence. When she first started attending the group, she was reticent about participating, but she soon overcame her reserve. She has used a journal extensively to help her through the healing process (see Chapter 7), but she has also written poetry about other aspects of her life, some of which are shown below.

In the Beyond Existing group Denise had always talked about her journal writing; it was only much later that she revealed that she wrote poetry and wanted to contribute some of it to this book. Her poetry covers many topics. She wrote numerous poems when she separated from her partner.

My Ex

The day you left me
My world was upside down
Why what was the score
You left me in hospital
You didn't want me anymore.

You stole my things
And you took it all
And now you're out there
You're having a ball.

You stole my things
Yes you stole it all
My videos, my books
My CDs and all.

Denise also wrote about the abuse she had experienced in childhood.

Being Hurt

I was a young girl
Who was hurt everyday
That's when I began to kneel and pray
That the hurt I was suffering
Would just go away.

The abuse I suffered
Didn't go away
The abuse that I suffered
He just made it stay
Then carried on hurting
Me in every single way.

Denise wrote many poems about her family members; both those who had harmed her and the ones she cares for now.

Mother

What is a mother?
I don't know anymore
Mine didn't want me
Didn't want me at all.

I wish I had a mother
Who loved me just for me
She didn't really love me
Or I wouldn't have been hurt.

Son

You are my sunshine
You are my life
I just wish you knew son
How much you light up my life.

You are my life
Each and everyday
Even though you are
So very far away.

You're so far away son
Each and everyday
And I sit and think
Of you in every way.

I sit and kneel
And then I pray
You're safe and sound
In every way
You're in my heart
And in my dreams
You're not so far away it seems.

Some thoughts from the poems

In discussion with the authors and in reading their work, we found that certain themes were important. First, victims of serious abuse sometimes need a considerable time to come to terms with events, and to clarify their feelings about themselves and those who have harmed them. Counselling should always be purposeful but may need to be leisurely in the sense that processes of healing cannot be hurried. In this respect, this work does not readily fit in to an ethos of social service based on simplistic definitions of task or managerial criteria of evaluation and success. As we have seen in the poems, we need to allow for 'two steps forward, one step back'.

Second, opportunities for writing about feelings and events may be especially useful for people who find difficulty in putting thoughts into words, or for those who have reached a stage where they need to take stock of themselves – taking stock in the sense of assessing how far they can put behind them some of their experiences, and how far they are ready to 'move on' towards new hope and new achievements. Writing is therefore an integral part of counselling, not a separate and unrelated activity.

Some writers feel that they gain support, additional to that provided by counselling, if they can share their feelings – verbally or in writing – with others who have been through similar experiences and who are similarly struggling to come to terms with them. A writing group should therefore not be devised simply as a recreational activity, even though (as the Reach Out Project demonstrates) recreation and fun may be an ultimate and desirable by-product of the resolution of inner conflicts. It is initially the provision of an opportunity to share private anxieties, fears and despair.

Not all victims of abuse need this opportunity: some do not need to share, as the act of writing is in itself sufficiently therapeutic for them. Without exception, we have found that the poems were written as a *private* outpouring of thoughts and that sharing, if at all, was a diffident afterthought. The desirability of sharing should never be assumed and groups should not be set up on this assumption.

In short, a writing group should be based on the assessment of individual needs: the need for privacy or for sharing; the need to extend the help given by individual counselling; the need to find words that may not come easily in face-to-face discussion. It is important also to recognise that, for some people, it is easier to express problems by the use of metaphor or by the description of symptoms rather than by direct definition or explanation.

Both in counselling and in writing, the sense of healing seems to derive from the recall of *specific* memories and events, rather than from a generalised statement of unhappiness or despair. Both in counselling and in discussing a poem, the counsellor should not too hastily express understanding: rather, the response should be one of *trying* to understand, and of seeking specific clarification of what is being implied. But this approach is acceptable only if time is given to permit specificity, and if the person being helped is aware of continuing, wholehearted and uncondi-tional emotional support throughout the process. Support is especially important as a kind of rest period after the disclosure of painful material: discussions should never conclude while the nerve endings are still exposed. It is true for all of us that we can bear the expression of pain only in small doses.

As some of the later poems indicate, the experience of abuse is closely associated with ambiguity and ambivalence of feelings. Blame towards the aggressor may be accompanied by personal guilt; and the guilt may be experienced as rational or irrational, depending on the precise circum-stances of the abuse. Furthermore, ambiguity or ambivalence may be accompanied by a kind of splitting within one's feelings: we have seen examples within the poems of a division between the 'devil inside' and the real self; there are examples too of the 'good' and 'bad' components of ambivalence being divided and attached to different people – for example, a good mother and a bad father – irrespective of their actual cul-pability. All social workers have worked in situations in which they are overly praised or unjustly blamed when compared with another important person in the service-user's life. Ambivalence is an uncomfort-able state of mind, and 'splitting' of some sort is often a means of comfort.

Thus, while one *accepts* what one is told or what has been written – it does, after all, indicate real feelings – one keeps an open mind on questions like 'what really happened'. It is our task, as helpers, not to pursue a forensic examination in order to discover the truth, but to encourage the expression of what is felt to be truth, and to stand by the victim while he or she seeks to resolve the logjam of feelings which prevents the achievement of personal integrity and the hope of a happier life.

An important question raised by some of these poems is the extent to which (and the sense in which) the recovery and defining of painful and degrading memories can be liberating for the victim. Some poems appear to descend into hopelessness (albeit only temporarily), while others clearly show how recovered memories can provide a basis for future growth. What makes the difference between these two outcomes?

A negative outcome seems to be associated *either* with those memories that are used to justify a presumption that the victim, prior to the abuse, lived in an idealised period of innocence, *or* with those memories that are used to emphasise and give permanence to personal suffering – the division between *my* victimhood and *your* fault. In contrast to this, positive outcomes from the recovery of painful memories seem to be associated with a search for understanding about one's own significance and wholeness despite the injuries one has received. How is this positive outcome achieved?

Several poems provide the key to this: namely, the achievement of forgiveness and acceptance – not, paradoxically, forgiveness and acceptance of the aggressor, but of oneself – that is, oneself and one's reactions in the context of particular past events. Initially, this process is one of fragmentation: events are reviewed piecemeal rather than collectively. But the memories then begin to cohere and to provide (as Indie Larma has put it) the rubble which can form a resource on which a new and stronger personality will be constructed, and from which new energy can be derived. Often, as we have seen, forgiveness and acceptance of the aggressor are not possible – at least for many years to come – but this does not and should not impede the search for self-acceptance and self-forgiveness.

For some writers, forgiveness and strength have been found through association with others in similar circumstances. Their acceptance of themselves has been based on three components: recognition that others have the same problems, hearing how others are making their own journeys towards a new life, and learning to accept and respect others who have been seriously damaged by events in their lives. Finding personal integrity and new hope lie not in identifying with popular heroes but with people like oneself with similar problems.

The poems have shown that healing can be a lengthy and intermittent process. Writing can be a useful part of this, but one that cannot be forced or hurried. And the patience, goodwill and wholehearted acceptance given by the counsellor or group facilitator are vital to its success. The complexity of forgiveness and acceptance has been usefully explored by Williams (2002). His approach is Christian, but his perspectives on the subject have wide relevance and application.

CHAPTER 7

Using Journals

To write or not to write

Not everyone likes to use writing as a medium of self-expression. There may be a number of reasons for this. Some people may have bad memories of school: for example, having to undertake spelling tests, write essays etc. There may be unhappy memories of being tested, criticised, ridiculed. It is important to note that these feelings are also sometimes associated with being abused and particularly with powerlessness in painful situations. Thus some victims of abuse may *not* find writing a useful method of working towards and through the healing process and a worker should be careful to recognise this. However, although some victims may at first be reticent when given the opportunity to write, they might actually enjoy it.

In this chapter the use of journals will be explored through the work that has been carried out in Beyond Existing groups and the work received from individuals from the Reach Out Project. Extracts from journals will be presented, which workers can use with other victims who may be thinking about writing a journal. Extracts are taken from the journals of Vera (age 67), Denise (age 40), Amanda (age 20) and Jo (age 19), some written as part of their group work and some in the context of individual counselling. Vera wrote a poem about her use of a journal (see Chapter 6, pp. 108–9).

What is a journal?

The *Oxford English Dictionary* (2000) defines a journal as: 'diary or daily record'. In therapeutic creative writing, a journal may have a broader use. It may be, but it does not have to be, a record of actual events and incidents, duly dated and timed. The writer may find wider uses for it, for example recording hopes and fears. The objective in using a journal in the healing process is that it will help the victim to express feelings about what has happened in the past, how they feel now and what they hope to achieve in the future.

Thus, a journal is for personal exploration and every writer will use it in a way that suits them. There is no right or wrong way. However, if a worker intends to work alongside the victim and help them through journal work, then ground rules have to be set (this will be discussed below).

Starting to use a journal

When a victim joins a Beyond Existing group, he or she is given:

- a book which is known as 'the journal'
- a small notebook in which to keep notes, jot reminders, e.g. dates of next session, what to bring, tasks etc.
- a plastic wallet to keep the work in.

A new member is told that the journal can be used in any of the following ways (see Handout 7.1):

- as a diary to record what has happened between meetings
- to express feelings from the past or in their current life
- to write the story of abuse (this is using reminiscence as a method of healing)
- to write stories
- to write poetry
- to write when participating in exercises (see Chapter 11)
- to use in his or her own way.

Handout 7.1, p.138

The focus of this chapter will be to look at how a journal can be used specifically in the first three ways mentioned above. The method of story writing will be considered in Chapters 8 and 9. Some members express doubts or fears about using a journal. Leaders should be conscious of the fact that some people may have difficulties with reading or writing and therefore may refuse even to contemplate using a journal. Jane, aged 70, was one such person. At her first meeting she said that she 'had never been good at writing', but with the help of a leader she did participate in an exercise that involved journal writing. When the leader contacted Jane a few days after the meeting to see how she was feeling, Jane said that she had started to write in her journal about the sexual abuse she had experienced in childhood. These writings have never been shared with the group and therefore cannot be included in this book. Workers must acknowledge that some victims will not wish to share their writing with anyone.

Survivors' groups may meet at different intervals – some weekly, others fortnightly or monthly etc. A journal is a way of remembering what has happened between sessions (especially if the meetings are only monthly). This is important in Beyond Existing groups because part of the agenda is to feed into the group anything significant that has happened between sessions; a member will state at the outset when the agenda for the session is being set if he or she needs 'special time' to talk about a particular issue. The journal can also be used as a vehicle to work on certain issues: for example, tasks can be set and then discussed at the next meeting.

Sharing

It has been acknowledged earlier in this book that people will write for different reasons and it is their right to choose what they want to do with their work. Some will want to share their work, others will not. However, if someone who has been abused decides to use a journal as a formal method in the process of healing, an agreement should be made between him or her and the worker about what will be done with the work, and how it will be used. For example, writing a journal may be:

- for cathartic use – sometimes just doing the writing is enough – the victim just needs to write their feelings down and has no need to talk about them

- a starting point for discussion and for expression of deeper feelings.

It can be useful for a worker to raise the following questions before the work begins (see Handout 7.2):

- What is the purpose in using a journal?

- How will the work from the journal be used?

- Will the work from the journal be shared? If so, how and with whom?

- Where will the journal be kept?

 Handout 7.2, p.139

Answers to these questions then form the ground rules for use (see Handout 7.3).

Ground rules for writing a journal

- Write when you feel like it.
- Write what you think and feel.
- Be honest.
- Never think your thoughts are trivial.
- Do not worry about spelling and grammar.

Ground rules for sharing

- You will only share when you feel ready to do so.
- You will only share what you want to.

- You will share with whom you choose.
- You will be listened to.
- Your work will be respected.
- You will not be criticised or judged.

Handout 7.3, p.140

When to write

A victim should never feel pressurised into writing. The journal should be used only when he or she feels it is appropriate:

31.10.00 Tuesday

Sorry to say I cannot concentrate on my journal.

Some may feel the need to use it every day; others will write only when there is a crisis. There is no right or wrong way to use a journal. We have seen elsewhere that Beccy writes her life story four times a year (see Chapter 6, Profile on Beccy).

Using the journal as a diary

It was said above that a journal can be used to record events between meetings. Writers are likely to use a diary as a recording tool in different ways. Some will literally just record what they do as part of their daily routine – this can give a clear insight into what their life is really like.

29.07.00 Saturday

Got out of bed this morning and like most Saturdays will be on my own and yet I do not mind. Well? It gives me time to think and I welcome that.

20.10.00 Friday

Laundry day again but I am feeling a lot better. My appetite is much better and it means no more soup and I can get some solid food.

22.10.00 Sunday

Well we are having a pork joint for lunch with veg and Yorkshire puddings. My first dinner for quite a few weeks and I know I will enjoy it.

23.10.00 Monday

Pension day again, and extra shopping to replace what we have used. We are spoilt for choice in freezer fridge and cupboards. Too much is better than too little.

After reading entries like this a worker can ask more about a person's life and how it affects them or can highlight what they want to change. Although Vera used the journal to express her negative feelings, she also recorded the good things that happened to her.

10.08.00 Thursday

What a day, to have a visit from my friend Ann. We met in [hospital] in 1999 and have been friends since then, she is a lovely lady we have quite a lot in common. As our marriages to Scots where happiness was nil.

26.08.00 Saturday

GOOD NEWS DLA [Disability Living Allowance] have awarded me the top benefit of DLA. I have a run of total downers, then things begin to change and good things begin to happen.

Vera chose to write about ordinary day-to-day events but she also included extraordinary events in her life as well.

16.09.00 Saturday

You are not going to believe this but it did happen. I had laid on my bed and started to catch up on my journal it was 7-10pm. At first I heard a screech of tyres then a very loud bang and two more. At first I froze. I went to the door. The street light was uprooted my handrails were no more, and a 5 door red estate car was perched on one set of handrails almost to the ground. Had the wheels not been trapped the car would have gone on its way into next door bungalow's front room. The police were very helpful as was the warden Jane.

Some victims will choose only to use their journal when something really major happens or they are in crisis. Denise used her journal in this way as well as writing about the abuse she had experienced, which eventually turned into her writing her life story.

Denise Writes About the Overdoses

I have taken overdoses while being with this man. Some serious overdoses. On the 14th December 2002 I took a massive overdose and I was on a life support machine. I left the hospital on the 21st December. I couldn't stand to be in the same place as him and I ended up in Churchtown Psychiatric Unit, Trinity 2. I am still there and today is the 7th of February 2003. I am in the same house when I am on home leave. I hate this house and am going to be rehoused somewhere else. I want to make a new start and have a new life without any abuse in any form. I have been going to a group once a month, which is like a lifeline to me. The people who run it are called Jacki and Janice. Without the group I'd be buggered. I have special people in my life and they are there for me. I also have the staff to thank on the ward, as they have been an absolute godsend to me and all who are included in my ward round. The people who pretend to be your friend aren't worth the friendship then there are the real friends who are there for you. My special friends are there for me and the staff who are looking after me on the ward have done more for me than my family have, and now hopefully I can forget the past and look forward to the future.

Using a journal to express feelings

A victim can write about how they are feeling and give a worker a key insight into the emotions they are going through. At one point Vera's self-esteem was extremely low because of her ill-health.

31.07.00 Monday

I feel utterly useless not being able to do things like going shopping and finding my own way around by walking without pain.

Her writing clearly expressed a whole gamut of emotions.

Boredom

02.08.00 Wednesday

Well as days go same boring routine get out of bed get washed and dressed take my medication after a light breakfast as I don't enjoy a cooked breakfast.

06.08.00 Sunday

Well I got the Sunday lunch prepared. The afternoon was boring so went to lie down for an hour and awoke 3 hours later refreshed.

09.08.00 Wednesday

I have got a letter from Newcastle so I can use some of my time to reply. Had a go on Lottery it is a rip off that is a fact. Went to bed after Trevor left for work.

19.08.00 Saturday

What a boring time I still have not heard about wheelchair or refund. My whole life has been one big disaster, and now well I have to get up a slippery slope on my own.

29.11.00 Wednesday

The day is dragging.

Monotony

14.08.00 Monday

A Monday routine never changes.

30.08.00 Wednesday

No change, the story of my life.

30.10.00 Monday

It is Monday routine as usual. What I need is a change of places and faces, if only

Hopelessness

08.08.00 Tuesday

A day like most days no place to go and no callers

Frustration

03.08.00 Thursday

Trevor went to Churchtown this week for our shopping. I get so frustrated I need to have a life as these four walls are closing in on me.

A worker must remember that dealing with memories and anniversaries is a crucial part of the healing work. Many victims will want to remember people whom they loved or who helped or protected them. A worker should endeavour to find out key dates in a victim's life and the journal may be a route to finding these out.

05.08.00 Saturday

Today is the birthday of my late father I was 7 years old in 1943 when he passed away. Owen and Rose popped in. Memories are so very precious as we grow older as is the love we received as a child. Marian called in she is deputy warden.

01.10.00 Sunday

My late mother and brother would have celebrated their birthday what a lovely twenty-first present my brother Bob was for my mother.

When something awful happens it can be embarrassing to talk about it. Vera actually lost a day of her life when she slept right through a day and was totally disorientated when she woke up and it was dark. The whole experience of losing time really frightened her.

23.08.00 Wednesday

As days go Owen is calling in for his lunch at 1-00pm and goodies for his snap it never fails to amaze me. I admit I do worry about him and always will. A strange thing is I forgot what day it was and why the sun was at the back in a morning 5-10pm.

24.08.00 Thursday

I am still wondering why I should be unsure of yesterday. It is not the first time I have lost track of time. It was a newspaper that convinced me. Could it be caused by being alone so much?

Vera's journal gave a clear insight into how her health declined over a specific period of time. She underwent a series of tests and in the journal she recorded her fears.

29.08.00 Tuesday

Don't feel so good my stomach sounds like a drain I feel terrible and it is like the drains need to be cleared.

31.08.00 Thursday

I have not felt well enough to concentrate

01.09.00 to 15.09.00

Got up but soon felt tired

06.10.00 Friday

They called for the doctor to visit. He gave me an examination and put me on a 7 day course of antibiotics. I feel no better. If anything the only thing I need to get well, could be better for me.

19.10.00 Thursday

I was seen by Dr Amin at the medical centre blood and urine have been sent to lab for tests. I am waiting for results.

24.10.00 Tuesday

I have to go to the doctors for test results 4.50pm Thursday.

25.10.00 Wednesday

I am feeling my nerves are on edge. I feel on edge about the tests and tomorrow I get the results fingers crossed.

26.10.00 Thursday

I have to book a taxi so far so good. Trevor is going with me. We got to the medical centre, and all I could do was look at the clock. Dr Amin called my name and so now I would know the test results. The urine test clear the blood well it showed a part of my liver is not doing what it should do. Now I am to have a scan and more blood tests. What a life.

27.10.00 Friday

The news has made me think and pray and call [social worker]. The news made me sit back and see how my life could be changed for better or worse.

08.12.00 Friday

Well the results are at the medical centre so I have to get the results. The scan showed I have scars on the liver, gallstones, and my left kidney is no longer functioning and is almost a nothing.

Denise had lived with her partner, Andy, for seven years. She referred to him as 'my rock'. However, after she had been attending the group for about 18 months the relationship broke down and Denise started to write in her journal about what it had really been like: that is, not the idyllic partnership she had portrayed. Through her journal writing she could tell the leaders and members of the group what she had not been able to express verbally. At this time, Denise was admitted to hospital after taking an overdose and in the following months experienced many different emotions. Her journal, like Vera's, gives a clear insight into her thought patterns.

Denise's Journal

18 February 2003

Well I am still getting upset all the time, then I feel better afterwards. I really have learnt that my ex partner can't have really loved me. I feel he used me for all of 7 years. I didn't often have sex with him, but that wasn't his fault that was due to all the other abuse I have suffered in the past. I just want to get on with my life and hopefully meet someone who wants me for what and who I am. Is wanting to be loved such a bad thing? I hope my ex partner and his daughter are very happy together, and rot in hell, they both deserve to rot. I certainly don't need shit like them. I've been through enough in the past two days. I have wanted to harm myself 3 times but didn't. I feel really proud not easy to pull back. I would like to take all those who have hurt me one by one and take them off the face of the earth.

19 February 2003

Got up felt hurt and angry. Just got on with the day best I could. I have cleaned my house from top to bottom. Just small bedroom to do now that my ex's daughter left in a disgusting mess. I am back at [hospital] tomorrow for my ward round, and I'm hoping for discharge and to be an out-patient. The doctors and the ward staff have helped me get back to how I am now, and can't thank them enough.

20 February 2003

Well haven't I done well. I have just been discharged from [hospital]. Without the staff, doctors I doubt I would have got through it on my own. The staff at my group have been there for me too as always. I got through that I have a fresh start now and hope I go far. Make a new life for myself. I am ever so pleased about the way things have turned out. I have a lot of my old friends and met some really nice people on the ward.

21 February 2003

Well world I got up this morning and felt really sad so I went for a walk down Station Lane and did some shopping. I was crying and feeling very very low. I felt so hurt and went to sleep for an hour. I felt a little tired but when I woke about an hour later I felt much better. I went to see the doctor at 3 p.m. and he put me on some medication. I took my first pill around 4 p.m. an within two hours I didn't feel down at all. I have done my housework again.

22 February 2003

When I got up this morning I felt down and hurt. A bit later I feel OK, a bit better than when I got up. Two of my daughters come to see me today. It was nice to see them.

23 February 2003

I got up this morning and I feel fine. I still hurt a lot but will get over it. I always do. I don't know how I do it but I get there. I am keeping contact with some of the people I met in hospital.

26 February 2003

For the past few days I have felt very hurt and very lonely. I have cleaned all my house down so that I have got rid of all traces of Andy. I have never loved anybody as much as I loved Andy. If only he hadn't got back in contact with his daughter I would still have been with Andy. We had been to hell and back but we seemed to work things out but all that is now in the past and I am now entering my new future. One day I hope to meet someone nice, but at the moment I am concentrating on the future.

2 March 2003

I really feel like crap today. Can't eat. My phone has gone to pot. I am really sick of life. My life from the age of 5 years old has been nothing but absolute shit. I don't know why I'm bothering to carry on living. I have seriously been thinking of ending everything. Yet again what have I got left beside family I don't see. I am used to being abused and I blame myself for putting up with it all the time. I don't see a future for myself, so why am I even bothering? What have I done wrong to have had such a rotten life. How much more shit do I take? I am frightened to go into another relationship in case I get hurt. My real dad used to touch my privates all the time when I was young. I thought that's what dads do and he used to hurt me loads of times. When I got older I knew that it was wrong But daren't say anything as he used to tell me he would bray [hit] me. You see he used to abuse me sexually and he used to hit me and hurt me that way too. He would really hurt me anyway he could. Then my stepdad hurt me in the same ways – sexually, physically and mentally. Sometimes I had to be in the same bed with him and my mum. I don't know why he did this. He has bullied my mum badly but why keep hurting me? My ex partner Andrew and someone he knows asked me why I let him do this to me. You see I had three children to my stepfather and my ex partner didn't believe in the end that it was stepfather's fault. They say they could understand it happening once, but three times was too much. But they weren't the ones who had to suffer all the time. It was me who was being hurt not them. I wanted to tell someone what was happening to me. I had a son nothing to do with my father or stepfather as there was a DNA test done about a year ago. When all this came to light in December 2001 the police were brought in. After I tried once again to take my life with a big overdose. I have in the past cut myself with a razor or a knife and taken lots of overdoses. In December, the 14th, I was on a life support machine because I took lots of tablets which my ex partner told me to take all. I came out of hospital on the 21st December 2002 and I went back home. I couldn't stand it but put up with being here as I had my son until Boxing Day. My son went home at 5 p.m. Boxing Day. By 10.15 I was on my way to Churchtown hospital. I was taken to Ward 2 and stayed there for 9 weeks. I am back home now but not feeling good at the moment. I am so fed up I don't know what I want at all. Hopefully one day I will be my normal self again. But what is normal? To me I don't know anymore. I want in a couple of months when I am a bit better to get a paid job and pay off all the debts that my ex partner has left me to pay on my own but I will do this and I will do it on my own and when I do I will get all the things I want to get and then save up. There are lots of people helping me at the moment. I have my group, my doctor, my consultant and my social worker. I just at the moment hate life and myself. It won't always be like this I hope. I have been told there is light at the end of the tunnel.

1 April 2003

A couple of weeks ago I found out that my two grandchildren who live in [city] have been abused by their father. Also my youngest daughter says the kids' dad forced himself on her for sex. All this caused me so much stress, that I cut the top of my arm to pieces with a razor. I had my social worker at my home with me till 7 pm and the crisis team. They all asked me to go to my GP the next day, so I did this. He put me on some more medication. I have not eaten hardly anything in three weeks, nor have I had much sleep. My best mate, Carol, stayed at my house last night to make sure I had a good night with no further accidents. When I spoke to my doctor I told him that I had made my mind up not to go to [city] to see my family. It was a hard decision to make but whenever I go over to see my family I get nothing but crap and all their problems. My ex-partner told me to do this many times before and I didn't listen. Them among other things destroyed my relationship. My GP agreed with me about my decision not to have any involvement with them in [city]. I have my son staying with me. He is the best out of the lot. My social worker has been brilliant also a godsend. I am mates with my ex-partner. He has also been a great help just by being there for me. I thought we were getting back together, but we decided to just stay friends. I am pleased that we could do this and if he ever does need anyone to talk to, I will always be there for him no matter what. Deep down I love him but that's as far as it goes. I have had a sleep this afternoon and I feel so much better. I have also been thinking about Jacki and Janice today and also Beryl, and the other two ladies Pat and Phyllis. So now I am trying to get back to where I was 4 weeks ago and I can do this, so Janice and Jacki you were right. I can and will do it as you both say I really do amaze you, as when I come back I'm so strong and no matter what I get there. So hey let's get back there, and with all the people I now have let the work begin.

5 April 2003

Well I got up at 7 a.m. today. Andy phoned me at 7.15. I was glad. I want to remain friends with him. He has a life to get on with. I have a life to sort out. I was talking to Sarah who is my oldest girl. I told her I was not coming over to [city] to them as I was sick of all the shit that they were giving all the time. I told her to tell Lisa and Keelie not to phone me again, as I've changed my mobile no. I would have got rid of my phone but I need it. It's the only thing I have to keep in touch with the people who matter at the moment – Jacki, Janice, my social worker, also a few close people. I feel a lot more confident this morning. I have my medication, the old and the new. I'm not eating properly, but that's going to take time, but I will get there. I am amazed with how I get through all this crap filled life. It is going better now that I have got all this sorted, and my grandchildren had their medical yesterday. They were fine and they have not been abused, and that load of lies could have got someone a lot of hassle and a long prison sentence. You see that's how sick my family are apart from my son. Well the least said about them the better, now going to get myself right.

Using a journal to disclose about abuse

Vera had been a victim of domestic violence but now she is facing financial abuse from her son Owen. Some victims will write about the abuse they are experiencing and openly talk about it; others will write in the hope that a worker will respond to what has been written without having to verbally disclose.

30.07.00 Sunday

Sunday a day of silence no visits from family not even a phone call. I am getting so used to it all yet feel like shouting to Owen and his wife get out and stay out I can't afford you anymore.

01.08.00 Tuesday

The day started slowly and the warden called as did Owen for the usual reason money. He is talking about a change of jobs I pray it will mean less visits.

Denise's primary purpose for using a journal was to write about the abuse she had experienced as a child and in adulthood. She wrote about things which she found hard to talk about, but once the journal had been read out by one of the leaders she could talk easily about the abuse. The account that follows was written when her ex-partner Andy had destroyed her journal and Denise felt it necessary to rewrite it.

Being Abused from the Age of 5 Years

When I was five years old I was abused physically, mentally and sexually. My dad used to tell me to get to bed all the time. He used to abuse and bully me, all the time. I was what was known as the black sheep of the family. I had three brothers and two sisters. My dad used to abuse me all the time, he used to make me stand on a sideboard and when mum came from town, on a Saturday, if I didn't tell her I was an Indian he would hit me bad. He has even hit me with a glass milk bottle, the abuse with dad carried on until I was around 17–18 years. Then came my stepdad. He married mum when I was 13 years old and had started to abuse me a few weeks later. I was in a children's home and was sexually abused, while I was either on holiday or I was on weekend leave. My mum was aware of this abuse, but I can understand why now she was afraid. She was beaten a lot of the time. I was abused by my stepfather. I had my son at 16 years old in April as I would have been 17 in June. I only got the chance to get into a proper relationship as my stepdad was sent to prison for armed robbery. But even from prison I was getting threats. When my stepdad did get released the abuse started again and did not stop until I was 24 years old. I never told anyone apart from my mum, who didn't believe me. How could mum not believe me when she was in the room some of the time. She too is full of crap. So my thoughts were if I can't be believed by my mum, who else would want to listen? I had three children to my stepdad. I wasn't allowed to talk to guys and if I did, I was beaten bad. He gave me black eyes, broken bones in my ankle and my nose was broken, I had cracked ribs. I was beaten once so badly. I crawled to a police station, but dared not go in, as he found me outside the police station he said if I told anyone he would kill my son and nothing or no-one was worth my son's life. My stepfather also at one time abused my son and my oldest daughter. My stepdad also once put a verse in the memory column, saying that my son had passed away. That's why I kept all my abuse to myself for 23 years. In my early years when I was 8 years old I was raped by a family friend, then raped again at 9 years old. I find it very hard to cope with all of this and tried to take my own life on many occasions.

In 1994 18th June I got married and I left him within 12 months. He was a drinker and started to hit me and I couldn't cope with it. Then in 1995 April 23rd I met a man who I have lived with for 7 years. He too was a bully. I have had a broken nose in two places. He once tried to set me on fire while I was in bed. This was because he wasn't able to cope without a fag.

Using a journal for exercises

Throughout her life Vera had written poetry and found it very easy to express herself in this way. When she started attending a Beyond Existing group, she was given a journal and she said she would see if she found it useful. Her first entry was about her objectives for the future which she had worked on in a group exercise during the first meeting (see Exercise 11.1 in Chapter 11).

12 months 28.07.00

To keep going forward and for my health to improve and be happy. Have a social life with friends.

5 years 28.07.00

I want to have grandchildren as part of my older years and have my sons to share my life's good or bad times.

Vera continued to use the journal and read it out to other members at meetings. Her entries capture very vividly (as we saw above) her frustrations and emotions through a time when she was experiencing ill-health and being financially abused by one of her sons, Owen.

Working on particular issues

When working with a victim it is likely that other issues will come to light that are linked to the abusive experiences. These issues have to be worked on as part of the healing process. For Vera the emotions related to the loss of her babies were an ongoing problem. Vera's husband had always threatened to keep her pregnant throughout the marriage. Vera had ten pregnancies, but only two children survived. She has written much poetry about the babies who died (see Chapter 6), but she also used her journal to express her feelings about her losses.

> *11.08.00 Friday*
>
> *Certain days of the year are important for me to recall the dates of babies I lost eight in all, but I do have 2 healthy sons.*
>
> *12.08.00 Saturday*
>
> *Monday 12.08.68 I gave birth to a son Michael 3lb 4oz. I will never forget him. So to-day has me feeling sad.*
>
> *15.08.00 Tuesday*
>
> *Another sad day my baby Michael died 3 days old. I still ask why me. I had no visitors as usual, 1968 was not a good year, for me it was yet another memory. They called him 'little boxer' as he had a black eye.*

Other journal work

The work from journals presented above was undertaken as part of a formal method of helping introduced in various Beyond Existing groups. What follows are extracts from journals from two young people who were part of the Reach Out Project: Jo and Amanda (see Chapter 5 for their profiles). Both women wrote spontaneously, not because they had agreed to do so in a group. The extracts illustrate different writing styles and different needs in expressing feelings.

Jo's Journal

Saturday 2nd December 2000

Well I have had a very sleepless and stressful night last night. I went out with Daria for a walk and Daria walked back on her own and I stayed in Manor Walks and I went into the Co-op and I bought 16 paracetamol and I went

*and talked to Peter and another cleaner and I told them what I was going to
do and I went at closing time, and I went to Allerthorpe and I was sat in the
office reading the paracetamol box behind a bit of paper, and I was asking
Barbara B what some of the symptoms meant and then I showed her the box
and I told her what I was going to do, and she tried to get the paracetamol off
me but I wouldn't give them her, so she said that if she didn't have them by
10.00 pm then she would start making phone calls. It came to 10.10 and she
gave me one last chance to hand them over and I walked out of the unit and I
went and sat by the bins and I sat there and took them all. Then I came back
in because it was cold and the staff were being nice to me, and I said that I
didn't know why and Barbara said 'you've taken them haven't you?' and I
said 'yes' and so she went into the office and rang the paramedics and they
came and took me to hospital in [town]. I had to drink charcoal and I had a
blood test taken as well which hurt as it was in my hand and not in my arm
like all the other times. After a night in hospital I was transferred to St
Georges and I had to see another psychiatrist and after she had consulted
her Consultant she said she didn't think that St Georges was the right place
for me and that she was sending me to [a unit].*

Monday 15th January 2001 7.25 pm

*I so feel like killing myself tonight. I am so pissed off but if I told the staff that I
was feeling like this then they wouldn't think so, because I haven't been
showing it tonight. I have been out to play pool with Chris, and I didn't really
enjoy it but I can't tell the staff, and it is getting to the point where I feel I have
to lie to the staff, instead of telling them how I feel. I don't like lying to them,
but also I don't want them to know how I really feel. I wish that I were
non-existent, everyone would be much better off without a fat, ugly, abusive,
ignorant slag like me.*

*Life just seems too much of a challenge for me to cope with at the
moment and I can't go on feeling this way anymore and no-one can will
believe it when I sometimes say I can't help it they just think I'm lying. Also the
psychiatrists say that I haven't got a mental health problem but that doesn't
mean I can't help it.*

Monday 22nd January 2001

*I took an overdose on Thursday morning about 1.00 a.m and I came in and
told Lesley (night watch). She asked me would I go to bed and I said well that
depends. If you want me to die then send me up to bed, but if not then call an
ambulance. She didn't take any notice and then when I said that I would call
my own ambulance, she still didn't do nothing and when I was on the phone*

to the paramedics she was stood laughing at me and shaking her head. The paramedics came and I was taken to hospital and Pat (staff nurse) was speaking to me for ages about my life and I got upset and was crying and she was really nice. Everytime I went into hospital with an overdose she was always there. I had my blood test taken and because I had taken 30 tablets my blood was dangerously high and I was sent down to the MAU ward and started on my treatment as soon as I got there I had the 3 drips again – 1) 15 minutes, 2) 4 hours and 3) 16 hours. I was really ill whilst I was on them because I hadn't had anything to eat. Wasn't proper sick it was yellow and green liquid. I met some really nice people while I was in hospital. Avril was really nice to me, she bought me things to eat while I was there and when I left gave me £10 and some sweets she was lovely. I spoke to Dr Morris on the Thursday night and she was going to send me to St Georges again, but I said no. She also said that I had mild depression and that she was going to put me on medication (anti-depressants). But I am not on them because Dr Taylor thinks I should work through my problems instead of relying on medication.

Amanda's Journal

Explanation

I'm going through a time where my heartache is not going away. The tears are always running down my face. My suffering feels endless. I'm certain I'll not be happy again. My heart is broken up in two. Why can't anyone help me? It seems people have turned their back on me. They can't care when I'm suffering. Even when I'm alone it seems like no-one is there for comfort or to keep me company. My real family have abandoned me. I cry myself to sleep at night. That's if I ever go to sleep. I'm always afraid. I feel like people are constantly looking at me. Why am I feeling like this? I need to know how to take my pain away. I'm smoking more than usual. Can someone help me please as I feel I'll only scream. Feel so alone and frightened that I really wanna kill myself now and I will do it eventually, one of these days in the very close run in a matter of a couple of weeks. I'm really sick of living. My life's been the same all the way through. DIE.

25.9.02 3.45 pm

Please Listen To Me

In your mind there's no escape of feeling love, feeling hate, feeling low sometimes and then feeling fine. Feelings of people letting you down, on my face I've got a frown. Needing someone to pick me up when I feel like s**t. Needing to speak to someone who cares, but they never seem to be there *when you need them, they let you drown I told people I've been there all before, I can't stand it anymore.*

Other writing

Finally, another piece from Jo is presented below. This is included in order to illustrate how writing can replace verbal dialogue. Jo was sitting in the cafe in the Reach Out Project with a group of other young people and a worker. She started writing notes to the leader. They continued the following written dialogue.

Coping

I'm always feeling down for no reason, what do I do?

Do you really believe there is no apparent reason?

Yes I do.

I don't believe you don't have the answers yourself, I believe you may need help to share the pain you feel and talking about why you feel depressed.

But sometimes I just feel so desperate and don't know what to do I can't see past the next few hours. I cry and cut up and don't know what to do to say to people to make them believe and see how desperate I am everything is so bleak.

This is different from not knowing why you feel depressed, what you are talking about is coping with how you are feeling. Reasons and coping with depression need to be separated so people can try and help you.

You're not much help are you?

What are you asking for?

I want to stop feeling like this and I want to stop feeling desperate.

Talking, taking medicine can help the feelings. However, understanding your life so far, understanding the pain this life has brought you, accepting this is not your fault, accepting you deserve better however only you can do something about feeling better. Your future is in your hands, your past was in the hands of others, let go of those hands, stop holding on to them, they are only leading you down into the dark.

Don't I know it, what help can I get to stop me feeling so negative and to build my confidence and self esteem, how long will it take?

It has taken you 18 years to form the person you are. It's understandable that letting go of the past will be hard as the past is you, but the future is also you. Change is scary, but the past is holding you back, it's blocking things out. Let go, put it in a box. You can become the person that in your dreams you know you want to be. It's all up to you.

What you say makes sense but it's so hard to let go of the past. I know that the things that have happened in my past have made me who I am and I shouldn't blame myself or torture myself because of it, but I can't help it.

You started this conversation by saying you didn't know why you felt like this? You have made such a huge step, accepting that how you are feeling is not your fault is so important. If you cut yourself it takes time to heal. Sometimes you forget what you cut yourself with, razor/glass? Adults have 'cut' you. Again these take time to heal, but in time you can try and forget them, the same way as the razor/glass. There are people who want to help you heal those hurts. Let those who care about you, care. But let those who have hurt you, go.

Exercise for workers

If journal work is to be shared with a worker or other members of a group, it is important to react appropriately and facilitate discussion. In order to practise this, this exercise can be undertaken by an individual or a group of workers who are thinking about undertaking journal work. The task is to read any of the extracts above and then answer the following questions (see Handout 7.4).

- What was your initial reaction when you read the extract?
- Did you read the extract more than once?
- What did you feel when you read the extract?
- What did the extract tell you about the writer?
- What did you want to say to the writer?
- Did you want to ask questions? If so, what were these questions?
- Did you want to do anything else?

- What issues would you discuss with the writer?

- Would you want to work on particular issues with the writer in future sessions?

Handout 7.4, p.141

USING A JOURNAL

A journal can be used for:

- Keeping a record of what has happened

- Expressing feelings

- Writing the story of abuse

- Writing other stories

- Writing poetry

- Exercise work

- Working in a personal/preferred way

USING A JOURNAL

Questions to be agreed between the worker and victim:

- What is the purpose in using a journal?

- How will the work from the journal be used?

- Will the work from the journal be shared?

- If so, how and with whom?

- Where will the journal be kept?

GROUND RULES FOR WRITING

- Write when you feel like it

- Write what you think and feel

- Be honest

- Never think your thoughts are trivial

- Don't worry about spelling and grammar

GROUND RULES FOR SHARING

- You will only share when you feel ready to do so

- You will only share what you want to

- You will share with whom you choose

- You will be listened to

- Your work will be respected

- You will not be criticised or judged

© Pritchard and Sainsbury 2004

JOURNAL EXTRACTS: QUESTIONS FOR WORKERS

Read the journal extract which has been given to you. Then answer the following questions.

- What was your initial reaction when you read the extract?

- Did you read the extract more than once?

- What did you feel when you read the extract?

- What did the extract tell you about the writer?

- What did you want to say to the writer?

- Did you want to ask questions? If so, what were these questions?

- Did you want to do anything else?

- What issues would you discuss with the writer?

- Would you want to work on particular issues with the writer in future sessions?

CHAPTER 8

Using Stories 1: Adults

We have seen in the previous chapter that a journal can be used in all sorts of ways. Denise chose to write about the abuse she had experienced through her life in her journal and in some ways her life story evolved through that process even though she did not consciously set out to write a story. Other writers consciously decide to write stories; such work will be the subject of this chapter. It may be useful for the reader at this point to reread the profiles in previous chapters (Chapters 5 and 6) regarding the writers Amanda, Jo and Laura.

Purpose in writing a story

Similarly to what we have discussed in earlier chapters regarding the use of poetry as a form of self-expression, writing a story can be a way of venting internalised feelings. It is also a way of gaining control. The abuser may have controlled the victim to such a degree that he or she feels powerless in many (if not all) aspects of life. One of the aims in writing a story can be to give a sense of control: the victim can write *when* they feel the time is right and will write about what *they* want – that is, without anyone telling them what to do. Bolton (1999) has commented that writing a story:

> ...clarifies orders, creates illuminating connections and makes contact with fresh psychological material. Once written, the story is

an object outside of the writer and can then be related to in a developmentally fruitful way. (p.105)

A common question victims ask is, 'Why did the abuse happen?' Many victims will blame themselves and a crucial part of therapeutic work is to help them understand that the abuse was not their fault. Following this, victims need to gain an understanding of why abuse can happen. Past events cannot be changed; it is necessary to come to terms with what has happened. In order to achieve this a victim has to work through how they view the abuse and what part it plays in their current life, and then place it somewhere in their future life. There is a need 'to create closure of our past and continuity into the future; through narrative a sense of coherence can be restored' (Etherington 2000, p.152).

Types of story

There are many different types of story and a victim of abuse may say, 'I just write what comes into my head', without consciously thinking in what way they are expressing themselves. Stories can take many different forms; at the simplest level they can be long or short. Most relevant in therapeutic work is the purpose in writing the story, but some consideration needs also to be given to the way in which the story is presented. When working with a victim of abuse the objective is to get the person to tell their story *and* to express their feelings, giving equal weight to both elements, and an equal sense of growing personal control.

Life story

A victim can set out to write a whole life story, which will include accounts of the abuse as well as other important events. One definition of a life story is:

A life story consists of all the stories and associated discourse units, such as explanation and chronicles, and the connection between them, told by an individual during the course of his/her lifetime that satisfy the following criteria:

1.   The stories and associated discourse units contained in the life
      story have as their primary evaluation a point about the
      speaker. Not a general point about the way the world is.

2.   The stories and associated discourse units have extended
      reportability; that is, they are tellable and are told and retold
      over the course of a long period of time.

(Linde 1993, p.21)

A writer will write in either the first or third person. We see below that
Amanda has written her life story in the third person as though it is about
someone else (though this 'slips' from time to time).

Life Story

By Amanda

There once was a little girl who never understood her life. She got
badly treated when she was young. She got locked in a bedroom
with her other sisters and was abused by her father and his friend.
This girl and her sisters were undernourished and not very well
cared for or loved by their parents. Her eldest sister, who was five
at the time, had to dress, feed and take two of her sisters to
nursery; while the youngest, who was this girl, had to stay with her
abusive parents. This little girl often wonders what had she done to
provoke such things. Was she a naughty child? She just didn't know.
Eventually the little girl's parents split up and herself and sisters
were passed back and forth from her parents. Often her mother
would stick them on a bus then her eldest sister would have to find
the way to her father's house after the bus driver told her it was her
stop to get off.

Her parents never once thought that these children could get
lost. The eldest sister, who was only five at the time, did a very good
job of looking after her sisters who were at the time 1, 2 and 3.

Eventually some time later their father put his children in this
home with some relative of his and they were even more badly
treated. So we were taken out of there by social services and stuck

---

in a children's home. By this time the little girl was three. The children's home was such a lovely place. The staff were ever so nice and treated them totally different from their parents. The children were never separated because people thought it would be in the best interest to keep them all together. This girl enjoyed living there and met a lot of people and friends.

This girl eventually went to school but got chucked out of class as she was very disruptive and she could never concentrate (maybe because she didn't feel secure).

By the age of 7, this little girl and her sisters got fostered by two lovely people who would do anything for you. This girl and her sisters wanted to stay there so they did. There were often meetings to see how these girls were getting on and the little girl eventually knew about adoption and kept asking to be adopted by these two people who also wanted to adopt these girls. They knew it would be hard work as these have gone through a lot.

At the age of 14 this girl and two of her sisters got adopted, the other who didn't get adopted didn't want to be so the two people didn't force her to.

Eventually as time went by there were a lot of difficult times and some very happy times. This girl, who was now growing up, started to go to counselling to deal with things from the past. It was often hard so she ended up stopping counselling.

The happiest time of this girl's life was when her niece was born when she was 15. Her niece was ever so special to her as she had recently miscarried due to rape, and she would never let anything wrong happen to her as if the niece was her own baby. She loved her more than anyone and anything else on earth. Her niece was ever so special to her now as her other two sisters had a baby but the sister, the one up from her, who had a son had to be adopted due to her problems and not being able to cope with a baby, and her other sister's baby got murdered at the age of 8 weeks.

The girl is now 20 and is going through a lot. She is going through a bad patch in her life. She miscarried again last June and is now going through depression, but at the end of it all, she wants to thank God for all the wrong stuff that's happened as she knows there will be a purpose for it and she will find out one day.

But this child of God knows no matter what you're going through, God is always there for you, even if no-one else is.

> **Comment from Amanda about her stories**
>
> *At the time of interview, Amanda said that she was tending to write stories rather than poems nowadays. Her advice to other potential writers is, 'Just write little bits at a time.'*

Life story books

Amanda's story is a short one. For some victims it may be appropriate to encourage writing a more elaborate life story book, which will take time. A worker who is supporting the victim needs to be conscious of this fact and the needs associated with it. It can be disruptive if a worker agrees to work in this way, the victim shares very important memories and feelings, but the worker leaves before the book and therapeutic work have been completed.

The value of developing a life story book is: 'It is a record of the past as well as a record for the present. It can be updated from time to time but the story is never fully told' (Gibson 1998, p.85).

Writers will choose how to present their life story book; there is no required format. Some will choose to include personal memorabilia (for example, photographs, letters, invitations, certificates, newspaper cuttings) which are not the subject of this chapter. If the reader wishes to pursue the idea of a life story book, he or she should refer to texts on undertaking life review and reminiscence work (e.g. Bornat 1994; Gibson 1998).

Autobiographical stories

A victim who writes in an autobiographical way will not be afraid to let the reader know that this is their story. Birren and Birren (1996) have developed a structured approach to individual life review in groups; they believe that there are many positive outcomes in working in this way, some of which would be very relevant to autobiographical work undertaken with victims of abuse, namely:

- a sense of increased personal power and importance

- the recognition of past problem-solving strategies and their application to current needs and problems
- reconciliation with the past and resolution of past resentment and negative feelings
- a resurgence of interest in past activities or hobbies
- the development of friendships with other group members
- a greater sense of meaning in life.

(Summarised from Birren and Birren 1996)

Thus, the key purpose in using the method of autobiographical story writing is that it helps to develop new perspectives. A worker may need to explore with the writer issues such as:

- blame
- forgiveness
- reconciliation
- reparation.

Other work and tasks may come out of the writing: for example, victims of abuse may decide they want to write a letter to their abusers or even decide to find or meet them. If a victim cannot face talking directly to the abuser, a technique that is often used is to help him or her say what they need to say to an empty chair, while envisaging that the abuser is sitting there.

Fictional

Some victims may not feel confident or brave enough to say that the story they have written is about themselves, and therefore they choose to write fiction. 'Fiction can be used to go on a fantasy journey' (Bolton 1999, p.112). Etherington says:

Sometimes it is easier for a person to tell their story 'as if', in the voice of a fairy story, or through a metaphor as a means by which they might draw closer and face their painful reality. In the initial stages reality might be too terrifying to fully experience.

(Etherington 2000, p.17)

Below is Laura's story, which is written as fiction.

The Challenge

By Laura

Katrina has been taking part in an award scheme with other young people from around the county...part of a developmental programme that she was 'encouraged' to join in order to 'be normal' and 'happy'. She is younger than the others and is a bit unsure at times whether she is good enough to join in the activities – she is tentative in participating and will often observe the others. If she does participate in the activities she is nervous and often tearful...but does not abandon the programme as she wants the award even though she fears the process.

The group are on a week long residential camp and it is day four, the group is on a 'treasure trail' and need to solve clues along the way – some of these are team challenges, some are individual.

Katrina has found an envelope on the ground as they rest beneath a tree, it appears to have been there for some time and the writing on it faded so no one is sure who or what it is. The others crowd round as she opens the envelope...torn pieces of a photograph fall out and scatter to the ground. She is curious and with the help of the others she puts some of the pieces of the photograph together in places that look as if they make sense. It is difficult however as the picture is so fragmented and much of it does not seem to fit together. Some large pieces are missing…and it is not clear from the picture so far what is on those missing pieces !!!

Katrina asks the others what she should do…is this picture part of the challenge…do we need to complete the photograph…is the photograph a clue which will help them complete the challenge? Will it matter if the photo is just put into her pocket and left…or thrown in the rubbish bin!!!

Most of the others think it is a clue and urge Katrina to complete the challenge, saying it is her turn to do some work !!! Jack doesn't see the point – it's a waste of time in his opinion. Jenna is a kindly soul who suggests that Katrina might get some satisfaction from completing the puzzle whether it is part of the challenge or not and urges her to do so. Ella shakes her head, calling Jenna soppy, and tells Katrina to get on with it and stop whinging, turning away to chat with the others.

Jenna reaches out to touch Katrina but Katrina shrugs her off and, setting her jaw, she walks off alone. She searches the ground around the tree…under rocks, in the long grass and under fallen branches. Jack gets impatient and tells her to 'get on with' this pointless task so the group can get on with the challenge. She finds a few more pieces, some of them are large and provide clues for the smaller pieces to fit in – some with no apparent link to the overall picture.

She feels like giving up, fed up with Jack either telling her what to do or sneering at her. She walks up to him to say something but he sees her coming and before she can speak he yells loudly at her calling her a 'lazy little cow' and raises his fist to strike her. The rest of the group look on. Katrina is terrified and when she cannot see Jenna she runs to a small cave set into the hillside nearby. It's dark and quiet – she feels safe. 'As long as they don't find the entrance…' Katrina mutters, 'perhaps if I am quiet enough they will maybe ignore me and go away'. She is however a logical girl and soon works out that sooner or later they will come and find her…her retreat will be found. She climbs though the entrance and walks down the hill to the others.

As she descends she sees a glinting object on the other side of the lake…only for a few seconds as a mist hangs over the lake most of the time. As she reaches the others Jenna and Jack say that they

too have seen something on the other side of the lake…it may be another clue to the challenge!!!

They encourage her to get the object but Katrina trembles with fear, tears rolling down her face, Jenna puts her arms round her shoulders, gently asking her what she is afraid of. Katrina babbles fearfully… 'But I can't swim, I don't know how to get there, what's in the water, it's deep and dark, I might drown…and for what????' Jenna continues to sympathise with Katrina…but this does not comfort her, soon sobs rack her body. Phrases occasionally are heard by the group… 'I'm pathetic', 'can't do anything right, he always said I was good for nothing!'

Jenna and most of the others crowd round encouraging Katrina but she takes no comfort in this. Their words and actions confirm to her how weak and useless she is because she is so afraid of the water. If others can swim so carefree then why does she have so much of a problem!!!!! 'I know I should do this, it's good for me!…but I can't.' At times she reaches for Jenna but then changes her mind…or sits up straight as a ramrod muttering to herself 'stop this, you have to get control!' …'Can't let them see this…'

Jack intervenes 'get on with it will you!!!' Then the mood changes 'Go away, leave me alone.' 'Fuck Off.' 'I hate this' – alternately Katrina sits with her jaw clenched and tears streaming down her cheeks or curls into a ball on the ground and is unresponsive, locked into her own little world. 'I am in control!!' she mutters. Occasionally an arm is raised and Katrina punches at the tree, bruising and bloodying her hand. She appears not to feel the pain despite the profanities emanating from her. The group stand well away, Jack appears unconcerned but the others are unsure and frightened at the obvious anger and distress. There is nothing they can do to comfort Katrina. After some time the sobs subside and Katrina slowly sits up and then stands…she makes her way towards the edge of the lake. She stands for a while trembling then turns and looks towards the others.

'Get on with it…' comes a sharp voice – it is Jack. Katrina wilts…she wants so badly to do this, to be accepted in the group, to have them respect her…but she is terrified of the water. She can swim a little, she's managed a width or two of the local swimming pool…but a deep, cold lake so wide???? Jack appears impatient and tells Katrina again to get on with it…since no other challenges have been announced then it appears this is the challenge. He says it's about time Katrina did her share and shouldn't be such a wimp, she must find a way to the other side…

Sheena offers Katrina a pair of arm bands which Katrina wavers about accepting… 'I shouldn't need them…' However Jason finds a small boat nearby and with the encouragement of the group  Katrina puts them on and steps into the boat. 'The only problem is that we cannot find any oars Katrina, you will have to paddle yourself' says Jenna. 'We will be around you in the water but we can't push the boat as well.'

Katrina gingerly begins to paddle and the boat slowly begins to move. Sometimes the boat rocks and Katrina freezes with fear. Although Jack shouts at her – 'don't be stupid it's easy!!!!! Just do it' the others encourage her and she begins to paddle again. Then Katrina smiles, she can see the shore…and begins to paddle strongly towards the shore. Then despair…Katrina feels her feet wet and looks down to see water lapping about on the bottom of the boat, there's a leak!!!!!

'What do I have to do?' Katrina shouts, 'It's not fair!' as she begins to cup her hands and slop the water over the side. Jack yells at her telling her to bale out. 'What the hell do you think I'm doing!!!!' she yells back as tears stream down her face yet again. 'Use both hands then,' Jenna encourages. Katrina shouts back that she's trying and weeps in frustration. She bows her head to try to hide her tears, she does not want others to see her – she wishes with all her might she was back in the cave…

Katrina becomes aware of new voices calling to her and slowly looks up. The boat feels as if it's sinking and Katrina hears a voice encouraging her to just jump out of the boat and swim to the shore she sees getting near. Katrina is frightened…she doesn't know how deep the water is…she could sink into mud, there could be strong currents to drag her under, she could panic and drown.

A voice comes from beside the boat 'I want my arm bands back Katrina…you can't have them any more.' Panic wells up in Katrina's body 'But I need them, you gave them to me, they are mine, please let me keep them…' Sheena is adamant, she wants them back. Katrina weeps silently on the surface and quietly reminds Sheena of her agreement… But in Katrina's head it is a different matter 'It's not fucking fair…I don't ask for much…I try always to be kind to everyone, I work hard, I think I deserve a little something just for me…why are people so horrible, why, after all I have been through can I not just have a little bit of life where I can be happy and not have anyone ruin it!!!!!' She feels like punching and kicking Sheena into a pulp!!!! 'Oh all right…' Sheena reluctantly agrees, 'you can borrow them for a bit…but I'll be back to get them in a few minutes…'

Katrina again becomes aware of the voice again which continues to urge 'you can swim – you have a 25 metre badge to prove it…just take the plunge, there are others around to support you.' Suddenly Katrina jumps over board…the sudden cold takes her breath away and Katrina feels panic arise, her stomach churns and she cannot move. Then a shudder runs through her body…and an anger so powerful floods Katrina's consciousness that it provokes her into movement…she breaks the surface and clumsily but steadily doggy paddles towards the shore. At times she feels she will never make it but she will not let them have the last laugh, how dare they make fun of her, break their promises…she is not weak, she will not drown, she will survive!

She begins to feel the bottom of the lake beneath her feet, it's a bit slippery at first but soon the mud turns to grass beneath her feet. She is surrounded by all her supporters, the others who had hindered her lagging further and further behind. Katrina reaches the shore and staggers to the shiny box she had seen from the far side of the lake. In it are several pieces of paper which, when put with the others, makes up a beautiful picture with a message below.

'Well done' the message reads, 'you have completed this task with courage, facing that which filled you with terror. Journey well as you encounter other challenges which may face you along the way and remember – you *will* find your treasures.'

Comment from Laura about her story

I wrote this story about three years ago whilst I was dealing with recurring nightmares and flashbacks of sustained physical, sexual and emotional abuse. I had suppressed most of these memories for about thirty years – there was no way I knew of then for anyone like me to talk to anyone about what had happened.

After one to one support I joined a group. After working for a while there, one of the ways suggested to me to realise how I felt was to write about how the process of working through the issues felt – without actually describing the factual events. However, the story had to have the kind of ending I would want…even if I did not think I could achieve it!!!!

At the time of writing the story I think I was about at the point in the story where Katrina's boat was sinking! This was the story that seemed to demonstrate how I felt at that point.

I have since reached the shore and opened the box.

Although I am currently facing another challenge I remember that I did complete that one. I realise I have the resources within me, as well as some of those around me, to complete this challenge – no matter how hard it appears whilst I am doing so.

If you are reading this because you have similar experiences, then I want you to know how sad I feel that you are. But if it helps you in any way to read this story – and perhaps inspire you to write your own story – then I am glad to have shared it with you.

I hope you find the way to your own boxes.

Reflective story writing

It has been said earlier in this book that, in order to heal, a victim needs to 'reflect back' on the abuse that has happened. Some people find that if they write the experience in story form, it is easier to reflect back on the painful feelings: 'Writing such a piece is illuminating and helps the writer move onwards and outwards from a stuck situation' (Bolton 1999, p.123).

Using this method is sometimes known as the therapeutic journey. Amanda wrote the following story when she was attending the Reach Out Project regularly.

From Bad to Good

By Amanda

About a year ago I used to go to college and work. But I dropped out of them both 'cos I was really fed up. I lived in supported lodgings (B&B type place) and wasn't coping very well. Eventually one of my sisters who I was living with at the time introduced me to the Reach Out Project. It's a brill place to go and chat when you're in a rut and can't cope. There's a lot of friendly staff who can really help. At first I only went a couple of days a week then eventually went all the time. I got to know places and meet new people. But deep down inside there was a lot going on in my head. Things about my past and why it happened to me. I was really hurting deep down and I just couldn't cope with it. I ended up taking an overdose and I ended up in hospital. I had to go back to my adoptive parents as the place I lived in didn't want me going back. Probably 'cos they couldn't cope with me. I eventually left my parents and stayed at my boyfriend's who lived in the west end. But I didn't stay there long. After that I went and stayed at my friend's house. It's a person who I went to church with. I stayed there a couple of months. Then I took another overdose. So back in hospital I went. The self-harm team came and saw me. After a couple of days in hospital I was allowed out but I was back in a bed and breakfast in [town].

I was often fed up, crying most nights, my head was feeling like a mess. While I was in the B&B I took quite a few overdoses, self-harm saw me everytime I took an overdose. Eventually I got a C.P.N [Community Psychiatric Nurse] and a psychologist who were really helpful. In spite of this I ended up taking my hurt out on my arm, which led me to ward twenty one, a psychiatric ward for people with mental health problems in September. I didn't stay there long but when they discharged me I wasn't allowed to go back to the B&B I was in, as my C.P.N thought I would cope better at my adoptive parents who live in [town], which is where I still am. I have now got a counsellor and I only see my C.P.N if I need to, although I haven't seen her for a month or so, but when I move in to my new flat I'm to phone her then. She's hoping that she can discharge me after my next review which is coming up shortly.

I think I've come on very well in the last year. Depression is awful but you do get through it eventually. You just have to think positive and keep saying 'I can get through this it's not gonna get the better of me.'

My counsellor said to me 'just because some people don't care, there are others out there who do.'

I had quite a bad early childhood, a murder in my family, and quite a lot more, but I've learnt not to dwell on the past but to think positive and think of your future. It may be hard but I am improving. Sometimes I have bad days but most people do. You just have to carry on.

I think of a little story which I made up, when I feel down, you know if you fall over in the street, do you just sit there? No! well most people don't do they?

Well when you feel like your gonna have a bad day or have a fall try and do something that will pick you up again.

No one knows the way your life is gonna be. There's good days and bad days but life does get better after you get rid of what's hurting inside of you, try it.

Try and talk to someone if you feel low and depressed 'cos people can't see through you. You have to talk it's the only way of getting your troubles out.

Here's another thing which makes me smile. I have it stuck on my mirror so I see it everyday. I am looking at the person who is responsible for making themself happy today.

Even if you find it difficult to talk try writing things down that's how I started getting all the bad stuff out. Writing poems, doing something positive makes you feel positive. Give it a try and think you can get through this.

It is hard but you just have to carry on. I hope this has given you some idea of what I went through but I'm coping just by taking one day at a time.

I have forgotten to write about Reach Out, that's where I go to talk about my problems. It's really good and it's confidential which is the best bit so the stuff you say will not get passed around. This has also helped me immensely.

Here is another story which, though 'reflective' in tone, indicates that the author has reached a stage of healing where the content of the story is giving way to solution and future hopes, and where earlier negative experiences are being transformed.

Carla's Story

No more hiding. I'm sick of hiding. I don't care if I feel the rain. I know life's out there, and I want to be part of it, live it.

I'm going to live, I know that because I'm strong. That spark inside of me, it's burning. Flooding my being with light that shines through the darkness, the pain. I'm not dead, I'm alive. I know that now. That spark, that hope inside of me reminds me everyday.

I can see life, the colours. I can feel the rain... I have tasted that, when it pours down, and your soul drowns day after day. But some days it washes over me, some days it's cleansing, pure. So that every raindrop fills me with joy and yearning.

I know so much, but there is still so much I need to learn. Like a child, reaching out to see if reds and purples will ripple at its finger-tips. Whether the world lasts forever, whether magic is real, or some distant song of knights and wizards.

I am a part of this world. Feeling the sun on your face...

We can be hurt so badly, but never killed inside. Here we are as immortal as time itself. All that beauty flows through us, that light inside, no matter how small... There isn't anything in the world that can take that away from us. Our dreams, our ability to feel, to love, we never lose that. Not really.

Sometimes we have to dig so deep to find it, sometimes blinded by the pain. Some days we can't find that spark, that light, and we are left in the darkness. But we are not forgotten. It's always there... even if we forget to feel it.

I have a destiny. I am part of this world and I will cling to it. I'll let my own light lead me through my darkness, my demons.

I cannot be touched because I know the truth. I believe in my strength, and I believe in my light, and as long as we do, nothing will ever break us, ever again.

When to write

An abused person may decide to write a story and then to share it when they feel ready to do so; that is, the decisions are spontaneous. In other circumstances a worker may deliberately introduce the idea of writing a story as a method of working towards and through the healing process. The worker may be working on a one-to-one basis with a victim or may be acting as leader in a group work setting. Some researchers in this field have asked participants to write at set times and regularly, in order to meet research requirements (Pennebaker 1988, 1993). In contrast to this, many of the writers in this book have said they have written when they felt like it. In our view, it is important if story writing is to be encouraged by a worker as an aspect of person-centred work that a ground rule should be agreed at the outset that writing must not be seen as a 'task' or 'homework'. The story must come naturally; it should not be forced.

We emphasise this because of the risk that where groups are utilising this method of working, there may be an expectation that members will write when attending the group sessions. Again it should be stressed that if a person does not feel like participating at a particular time then that will be respected. It has to be acknowledged that there are times for all of us when we do not feel like doing something; and if forced we probably do not perform well or produce our best work.

It may sound very formal, but we believe that a worker should discuss these various issues with the individual or group and develop a contract or agreement so that all parties are clear about the objectives of working in this way and within what boundaries they are working.

What happens to the work

A worker will want to use story writing in a constructive way. However, one has to remember that the story belongs to the writer. Therefore, as stated above in regard to developing a contract, agreement needs to be reached regarding how the story will be used in the therapeutic process (see Handout 8.1). Basic questions to be considered jointly are:

- What is the purpose in writing the story?
- How will the story be shared (read out loud or silently)?
- Who can read the story?
- Who can listen to the story?
- How will the story be used?
- Where will the story be kept?

Handout 8.1, p.160

Giving support

Writing a story is a cathartic experience and when the story is linked to abuse, then a worker needs to be ready to give emotional support to the writer. A writer can experience a wide range of emotions during the process of writing the story. We have seen in previous chapters that some writers with a history of self-harming have done so even when writing a story. If a worker is present when a writer starts to show strong emotions, he or she needs as a matter of urgency to offer willingness to listen to the writer and encouragement to verbalise distress.

Support may also be needed if the writer decides to share their story with others. Some writers may feel strong enough to read out their story in a group or to an individual worker. Others may ask someone to read the story aloud on their behalf or they may want a worker to read the work privately. It is crucial that the worker reacts to and validates the work. It is pointless if the worker just sits and listens without any response. The objective in using story writing in the healing process is to acknowledge the presence and validity of painful situations and feelings, and – when appropriate – to help to put them in some sort of order. Therefore, it can be helpful to establish some ground rules about writing and sharing. The reader should refer back to Chapter 7 and Handout 7.3.

STORY WRITING

Questions to be agreed between the worker and victim:

- What is the purpose in writing the story?

- How will the story be shared (read out loud or silently)?

- Who can read the story?

- Who can listen to the story?

- How will the story be used?

- Where will the story be kept?

CHAPTER 9

Using Stories 2: Children

The Open Door Project is concerned to promote the well-being of children, particularly those who have suffered serious abuse. Various activities are undertaken in order to meet this concern: individual and group counselling with children and parents; a writers' group; art and play therapy; and training and consultation for carers and for colleagues in other services.

This chapter illustrates how stories initiated by children can be used to help them find ways of expressing experiences and negative feelings, and to achieve some sense of personal control over the continuing emotional effects. This chapter focuses on stories devised in group activities, in which the aim is to find modes of expression relevant to the experiences and needs of all the children, both individually and collectively. The stories are, in essence, made up of symbols, metaphors and analogies which individual children can apply to themselves while at the same time recognising the similarities within their various experiences and feelings, and the help they can gain through sharing them with others. Abuse is a lonely and isolating experience. These stories help to reduce loneliness and isolation; they indicate how some sort of recovery from past damage can be collectively as well as individually achieved.

Initial procedures

The children who attend the groups are often on the Child Protection 'At Risk' Register. Acceptance into the project is based on an assessment in which one worker meets the child, and another seeks the views and needs of adults and other children involved with the child. A case history is prepared and suggestions shared about how the child might best be helped – for example, by individual or group counselling, by art and play therapy, by counselling for parents and/or carers. An agreement is then drawn up with all the parties concerned.

In the agreement with the child, explanation is given about the number and timing of meetings, the availability and use of the playroom and toys, and the 'boundaries' or ground rules of group meetings: for example, that children must not hurt each other, and that the group leader will always intervene if any child feels hurt or harmed. Some children participate in both individual and group work, and it is important that they realise that the two activities have complementary aims: a child should not feel confused about whom to talk to about what, particularly when one recalls that sexual abuse within families is usually accompanied by secrecy, guilt and fears about disclosure to one or other parent.

The children's groups in which the following stories have been developed and used take place within a framework of parallel activities within the Open Door Project: contemporaneous work with mothers, especially those who are still in touch with (or living with) abusive parents, on how to ensure the future safety of the child; support and information to parents about the effects of sexual abuse, both on the child and on themselves, and how best to address their own emotional needs; supportive work with foster carers.

In this complexity of complementary forms of help, the role of the leader of the children's groups is of great importance, both as a therapist and as a source of understanding for others about what is being achieved: why story-telling, fantasies, acting and play are constructive contributions to the children's present and future well-being, despite the apparent 'distance' of their content from the current domestic or legal situations.

Anna, the group leader, is a psychodramatist, trained in counselling and social work. In addition to child protection work, she has provided help in the Sexual Behaviour Unit of the local probation service, and to prison staff in respect of health issues affecting teenage boys in a Young Offenders Unit.

Child-centred work and its limits

Anna's work with the children's groups is child-centred in two distinct ways: in terms of purpose and in terms of process. The purpose is fourfold:

- to make sure each child is and feels safe; this is of paramount importance

- to offer time and space for self-expression, particularly of ambivalent feelings

- to foster in each child some sense of control over his or her private and domestic world

- to raise self-esteem.

The process of the groups is child-centred in that Anna follows the children's agenda at their meetings. There are, however, certain understood and agreed boundaries: that other children must also be protected from harm; that the leader will periodically switch roles from playmate to leader; and that alternatives to disruptive or wild behaviour will be worked out. Thus, the children are helped to understand when Anna is a playmate and when she is taking control ('This is Anna speaking'). Alternatives to disruptive and potentially chaotic behaviour are often found through the child and leader jointly devising the performance of symbolic or compensatory rituals. (We do not have to look far to find adult equivalence and institutionalisation of the control of wild behaviour by means of rituals.) In the present groups, one boy ritualistically sings a song before he leaves the playroom (which he had previously wrecked); and one of the girls has to have a wedding ritual before leaving. In short, the notion of child-centred work is not related simply to the intentions and skills of the helper; it derives equally from the suggestions and directions of the children, and from agreements about purposes, roles and behaviour.

How the groups work

Anna describes the work of the groups as a series of steps starting with art-work: the children talk about their own and each other's paintings (the meanings, *not* the quality); they accompany talk by actions in order to make the meanings clearer; they share reflections on common themes; they develop a story line/scenario which relates to all the paintings; they act out the story; they think about what they have learnt which may be relevant to their immediate situations. Although these steps or phases appear to form a neat sequence in theory, practice shows the need occasionally to go back as well as forward, to repeat certain key stages, to spend sufficient time in making up a story to ensure that it feels relevant to all members of the group. The enactment of the story usually takes place more than once, in order to ensure that its cathartic and cleansing effects are experienced by all the children. Final reflections always need more than one session.

The girls' group

At the time of our visit, the girls' group was made up of Catherine and Francesca, who were living with their families, and Emma and Sinead, living with foster carers. Their ages ranged from 10 to 14. It was possible for us to interview Emma and Sinead, and both have already appeared earlier in Chapter 4. Emma, who is quiet and shy, found it hard to explain what she particularly enjoyed and gained from the group: she liked all the activities. But the key thing was making friends: 'You can talk to each other, understand what they have been through.'

Both Sinead and Emma thought it was important that they had cried together. Emma said she often 'came in sad, went out happy'. Being able to express their feelings was very important to all the group. Sinead talked about other feelings (for example, anger) she had experienced during the sessions. She was honest about how she had sworn a lot during one session: 'I was pissed off. I talked about it and felt better.'

The story work

In the girls' group, work was undertaken in three structured phases. First, they undertook drawings or paintings which related to their abusive experiences: they made masks, drew pictures of the person who had abused them with explicit (and often horrific) drawings of what they would like to do to him or her, and they talked to each other about what was the worst part of the abuse. Some of the drawings did not survive; they were destroyed. Sinead said that she also drew what she wanted to do to her stepbrother who had abused her.

Issues produced in one group session

- I thought I was going to die. (Francesca)
- I didn't know what was happening. Not telling my mum straight away. (Catherine)
- When Dad told me not to tell anyone. Keep it a secret. (Sinead)
- When Dad was hitting me and I had lots of bruises. (Emma)

They then decided on a story line, and painted a collective picture to set the scene. People who had hurt them were translated into animals: 'If Dad was an animal, he would be a ferret.' The girls then drew a family group with no faces. When Sinead was interviewed about her experience in the group and the work produced, she said about the picture and the scenario: 'I felt a bit scared at first. I did not want to show my feelings. After, I felt happy and I really wanted to show my feelings.'

Following this there was a lively discussion to put together the details of the story. With Anna's help, the story was slowly structured into three components:

- what was happening
- what needed to be done
- how it can all end satisfactorily.

Parts were allocated and the story was enacted (always more than once, and always with exciting additions and adaptations).

Finally, there were discussions of how it went, how everyone felt about it, how there will be better things to come. Each phase lasted for three weekly sessions. Anna commented: 'The whole process of nine meetings is one of working with and through metaphor.' The following story formed the core of the work in the girls' group and it illustrates the essence of the three phases of therapy.

The Heroine and the Helper

Sara is 13 years old, she lives with her mother Marie, her father Warren and her brother Terry who is 4 years old. Terry is a little rascal, he is always up to mischief, he back chats the grown ups and gets himself into trouble at school.

Sara's parents shout at each other a lot and they don't discipline the children at all, they just let the children do what they want. Sara's grandma Ellen is however a sensible woman and so sometimes when Sara gets upset she runs away and goes to see her grandma. Grandma is always kind to Sara.

Sara doesn't like living at home with her mam and dad, she doesn't like the swearing, the shouting, the arguing and the beatings. Terry is the favourite, he can bring his mates home and do what he wants.

On the day that our story began Sara was at home, in her bedroom, her brother Terry was in his bedroom, mam and dad were downstairs. Sara could hear them from her bedroom; they were as usual, shouting and screaming at each other. Terry was running in and out of her bedroom annoying Sara, she called and called to mam and dad but they wouldn't come. Eventually mam screamed at Sara to stop the noise, as usual she got the blame. Dad called to Terry and gave him some sweets while Sara was told to be quiet. Sara ran off to grandma's house, grandma's house was warm and friendly, her grandma always made her feel welcome. Sara stayed with her grandma for a while and then grandma told her that she would have to go home.

Sara's mam went out that night and Sara was left alone with her dad and her dad sexually abused her, he dragged her into the bedroom, 'don't be scared' he told her 'I'll not hurt you. It'll only take a little while, don't tell anyone or I'll do it again and again.' Sara is hurt lots and lots of times by her dad, in her bedroom, her brother's room, mam and dad's bedroom, the only safe place for Sara was the kitchen.

Sara was upset, she was so angry she felt she wanted to kill dad. She wanted to tell someone, she was very embarrassed and emotional. One day Sara decided to take a chance and tell mam but her mam got very angry with her, she hit her and said 'Don't say anything about your dad he is a nice man'. Sara felt angry and stupid and decided to run away again to grandma's house. Sara felt it was her fault.

Sara was upset when she got to grandma's house. Grandma asked her what was wrong. Sara told her what dad had been doing and grandma said 'You tell me if he does it again' then mam and dad came and took her home.

After Sara left her grandma began to worry about Sara and she decided to go over to the house and talk to Sara's mam. She told Sara's mam that she was going to call the police and she did.

The police came to the house and Sara told them what her dad had done to her. The police arrested her dad and took him to the police station and he was questioned by three different policemen. Dad said that Sara was telling lies and that he had not touched her, but the police believed Sara and they put her dad in jail for the night. Sara was taken to see a doctor and she was examined.

The next day dad was interviewed again and he still said that he had not touched Sara but the police did not believe him, they believed Sara and he was thrown back into jail. Later that day dad admitted what he had done to Sara and he was put in prison.

The group is now planning to write a book, which besides setting out their collective story and their feelings about events, will also contain 'pointers' for other children. We list the headings here, and look forward to discovering how in due course they elaborate them:

- Trust someone
- How to get in touch
- How to get on with your life

- If no one believes you, tell someone else
- Never be afraid to tell the truth to people you can trust
- Don't listen to people who hurt you
- Don't bully them [*sic*]. Don't believe what they say
- Never ever talk to strangers
- Trust only parents and known adults.

The boys' group

A similar group was offered to boys aged 8 to 12 years who had been sexually abused. The objectives in running the group were to:

- offer a place where boys could meet with others who had similar experiences
- share worries and confusions
- ask questions and have them answered
- offer a place where they would be respected and listened to if they needed to talk.

The group met on Saturday mornings for four weeks from 10.00 am to 1.00 pm. At the first meeting the boys decided that in order to feel safe they needed the following ground rules in place:

Ground rules

- The group is private except if someone tells us that they have been hurt or harmed. Then the group leaders will protect them.
- We don't hurt each other.
- We won't say things that hurt each other.
- We will meet four times on Saturday mornings.

The group processes were led by the boys and determined by their needs; they decided how they could best get to know each other and devised games that they could play in order to facilitate this. Once safety was established the boys began to move into action and used metaphor, story and actions to deal with their problems and externalise their feelings.

Initially the boys worked out a story about the castle – a place where wars were waged over ownership and good battled with evil. Then they made sure that the people who had been hurt were taken to hospital and from hospital to a safe place.

A new story about James Bond followed quickly based on '007 kills the bad guys'. The boys planned to make a video. In Scene 1, 007 goes on a mission to protect people and travels to different countries and places. In Scene 2, 007 kills the bad guys while the others continue to take care of the hurt people.

Themes of hurt, injustice and powerlessness slowly began to emerge. No matter what was tried, the bad guys always won, until at the next stage, the therapeutic process was wrapped up in a final story about '**THE JUNGLE**'. All of the boys would come together and together kill the monster.

This was played out in a large room at the top of the building. The boys used art materials, toys and whatever else they could find to create the jungle; it was a place where snakes, beetles and other creatures lurked in the shadows. The boys moved into action and played out the following story of resolution and success.

Moving into action

The scene was set and the boys began their journey. They wandered through the jungle stepping over beetles, snakes, spiders and other creatures until they came across a huge tree. As they stood and admired the tree, something came up from the roots of the tree and sucked the boys in, the boys struggled and struggled to get out of the tree and the group leaders tried to help them in the struggle. But no matter how hard they tried, the leaders could not rescue the boys.

Sometimes the monster would spit the boys out and they would try to escape and the leaders would try to rescue them but always the monster pulled them back. The leaders felt helpless and said, 'We are never going to be able to rescue the boys; each time we try the monster just pulls them back in.' So the leaders sat down on the ground, feeling defeated. Suddenly the monster gave an enormous burp and all of the boys shot out from under the roots of the tree; they jumped up, grabbed their weapons and demolished the jungle, the tree and all that lived beneath it.

The work was then written up in the following story by the group leaders after the meeting, and shared with the boys.

The Jungle

In the Jungle there was a big tree and a snake and a parrot were in the tree.

A monster hid behind the tree and kept sucking the boys in. No matter how much or how often people tried to save them they couldn't be rescued.

Then one day after the monster had spit the boys out again and again it gave out an enormous burp and the boys shot out of the monster's mouth. The boys suddenly became quite strong. They got their swords and hacked their way through the jungle, hacked down the tree and killed the monster.

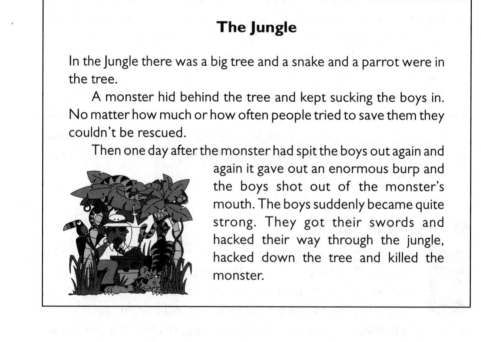

Evaluation

The boys evaluated the work at the end of the group sessions. They did this by producing the following picture.

Figure 9.1 Picture by the boys' group

CHAPTER 10

Endings and Beginnings

This book has brought together the activities, plans, experiences, fears and hopes of many people – not least of ourselves, acting as compilers, recipients and editors of a great deal of personal material. Some has been painful, some shocking. All of it has contributed to the humbling experience of seeing how well human beings can often cope with traumatic experiences in their own lives and, in the case of the group facilitators, with traumatic events in the lives of others.

It is impossible, and probably unnecessary, to devise a neat final chapter entitled 'Summary and conclusions', or some such. There are too many diverse strands, not all of which can be convincingly woven together. Furthermore, we want our co-authors' writings to remain vivid in the memory, in all their starkness, rather than neatly tucked up in a blanket of editorial conclusions.

Nonetheless, there is one theme that, just as it made the book possible in the first place, can properly be reintroduced at the end, as a final piece of advice from our contributors. The theme is 'Sharing: the costs of mutuality'.

Amanda has a typically in-your-face challenge to the would-be sharer.

STUFF
By Amanda

I'M SITTING ON MY BED
BORED OUT MY HEAD
WISHING I WAS DEAD.

I CAN'T CONTROL THE WAY I FEEL
AS I'LL ONLY SCREAM
PEOPLE ARE GETTING ME DOWN
I WISH THAT I COULD DROWN
OR SWIM FAR AWAY
FROM ALL MY PAIN.
I DON'T THINK PEOPLE CAN COPE WITH ME
THAT'S WHY I'M STILL IN A B&B

Amanda is sharing something with us, albeit reluctantly. Does she want us to share anything with her?

This book has been based on the willingness of people to share their experiences. For most writers, their intentions at the time of writing were to achieve feelings of inner relief rather than to share these feelings with others; indeed, some have destroyed much of their work rather than share it, partly because of its essential privacy and – in some cases – because of its potentially damaging effects on members of their families. But for others, sharing what they write with other people has been an essential aspect of the healing process.

We found no examples of indiscriminate sharing, however; if it happens at all, sharing is a highly selective process based on the writer's assessment of another person's willingness to listen, rather than to comment, and to accept what is written rather than to interpret or edit it. Editing and commenting were experienced by some writers as damaging to the integrity of what they had written or as attempts at reductionism.

We have been dealing therefore with high levels of sensitivity and privacy, and with the need to respect and protect the inner space of people's personalities. Writing for therapeutic purposes is not primarily intended for sharing with others, except when the healing process can, in the writer's mind, be a guaranteed outcome. As this book represents a public sharing, its very existence is based on the writers' individual decisions to try to help others in ways that they have personally found helpful. These decisions were not taken lightly; they represent for several contributors the antithesis of self-advertisement and self-regard; they represent an uncharacteristic willingness to display vulnerability.

We stress this point for two reasons: first, it indicates the complexity involved in setting up a writers' group for people living with traumatic experiences – or in encouraging any such persons to commit their feelings to paper; second, it offers a starting point for considering what, in this context, are the nature and limitations of sharing.

In therapeutic activities, to what extent is sharing a two-way process? What, if anything, should the helper also share of his or her thoughts and feelings?

Alan Keith-Lucas (1972) wrote that a helping relationship is mutual, not one-way, in that both people bring something to it. But it is not simply a *comfortable* relationship between people. In the helper, it requires self-awareness, self-criticism and self-discipline. It requires being able to face the reality of another person's feelings without false reassurance, to offer support when the situation seems threatening and hopeless (as in Amanda's poem at the start of this chapter).

In so far as a piece of writing is, in essence, a private expression of needs, feelings and experiences, it should be regarded as unique. No person's feelings can be wholly recognised, understood and shared, because all feelings are uniquely experienced. Thus, even though invited to do so, a helper's attempt to express sympathy and understanding by referring to a personal parallel experience misses the point. The most one can say is that all people in difficult situations experience feelings which need to find expression and to be accepted, but that no two sets of feelings are identical; they cannot justly be compared or set alongside each other.

One is reminded of similar pitfalls in giving advice to people. In response to wholly practical questions, one can appropriately give practical advice: where to go, whom to see, what resources are available. But when it comes to helping others in situations evoking strong emotions, advice is usually unwanted and even resented – often, paradoxically, even when it has been asked for. If feelings are chaotic or ambivalent, no one is more off-beam than the kindly person who says, 'If I were you...' or 'If I were in your shoes, I should...' Most social workers, in weak moments, have given advice of this kind, only to be met with the response, 'I've done what you suggested, and it didn't work.'

So sharing one's own experiences needs to be rationed and viewed with a sceptical eye. We need to ask ourselves, 'Why do I want to talk about my own life? Will what I say really help? Or am I merely expressing a sense of my own helplessness when confronted with another's pain? Am I merely offering a pretended companionship, rather than a truly helpful response?'

Sometimes, of course, one is asked direct questions: Are you married? Do you have children? Has anything like this happened to you? Have you ever tried drugs? Are you gay? In most situations, most of us love talking about ourselves, and the sort of work we do probably indicates that we are outgoing people. For some – perhaps many – of us, our willingness to work with and to be identified with people suffering severe hardships is bound to raise the question: are we really so saintly, or does our work represent the fulfilment of inner needs which, on the whole, we would prefer not to explore? So, in answer to direct questions, rationing is again the starting point, followed by a further enquiry. We suggest a straight, calm and honest answer, but a friendly enquiry whether the answer is what the questioner hoped to hear, and whether the answer 'matters'.

It is useful also to remember that a helping relationship continues *between* meetings. We certainly expect that the person we are attempting to help will continue to think about our discussions. So also, if the relationship is a truly mutual one, we continue to experience the understanding, respect and 'genuineness' which we hope we have displayed in the presence of the other person; we continue to think about her or his situation and responses; and we reflect also on the range of explanations and theoretical constructs which may have relevance in our next encounters (see Coulshed 1991; Payne 2002).

We hope that the writings that follow will provide opportunities to think about their significance, and to consider how we would respond if they were given to us by the writers. We noted earlier that all the writings printed so far in this book were selected by the writers in discussion with us; but they allowed us also to keep other work for publication without commentary. We are glad to present this material, in the hope that it will be used for private reflection or for group discussions (among workers, or perhaps with members of other writing groups or support groups for survivors of abuse).

The writings are not presented in any particular order. But their authorship is attributed so it is possible to compare different works by the same author.

Dirty Bastards
By Jo

Sick of people taking advantage,
Why don't they listen to me,
When I say 'no'!
They think no means yes!

They're all dirty bastards.
And deserve to rot in hell.
But they can't,
Coz that's where I'm going.

They made me feel dirty,
Made me feel like scum,
Made me scared of men,
Which isn't my fault.

They took away my years,
And I'll never forgive them for that,
People did believe me when I told them,
It's not my fault I had bad luck, IS IT?

Bed Blood!
By Jo

The blood comes from my arm,
Taking the badness with it.
It'll go away some day,
And I'll keep cutting till it's gone.

The blood is red.
Red as my anger and pain.
My blood should be black,
Black for all the badness.

The blood seeps through the cloth,
Till the cloth is red too,

Red is forever,
The blood that is good.

People don't understand it,
But why should they
You can't understand what you don't do,
It's not bad it's good.

You
By Amanda

I try to go to sleep at night
But I always end up having a fright
I'm thinking most of the time about you
Oh how on earth could you.
You've put me through pain when I was younger
Now I'm getting the pain again now I'm older.
Memories don't just fade away
I'm needing somebody help it fade.
The abuse you put me through has made me mad
You controlled the things you had.
I was only a child, remember that
So why on earth did you do that.
You've made me angry and afraid
That I can't behave
Behave like an adult should do
But instead
I'm thinking
Thinking of you.
Oh just can't you see
That I want to be me.
My head's messed up with stuff from the past,
Which all came to me as a blast.

Die Please
By Amanda

Death is what I want
I need it right now
Everyone probably sick of me.

Please let me die
Love is never there anymore

A person who is angry
She tells me how to kill myself
Everyone says they care,
But I don't think they do.

Life is S**t
By Amanda

Love is not there anymore
I am always remembering the past
F**king s**t heads are my birth parents
Everyone seems to like me
I try and take an overdose to die
But it never works
S**t is what my life is made up of.
Happy – never
Always angry with myself
I want to die
So why can't I?
The life I have is not worth it.
My parents have hurt me so much
I wanna die.

Things
By Amanda

Things are getting me down all the time
I'm really sick of life.
I'm really messed up in the head.
I'm fed up all the time.
There's never anything to do.
I feel like crying but I can't let it out.
I can't talk to people about my feelings
Or I'll do something daft
I try and kill myself
But it never works.
I dislike my life
My parents have wrecked it
People say forget about it
But how can I forget those awful memories
I'm really sick of life.

Free
By Amanda

Can't you see
I wanna be free
Free to do
What I wanna do
I wanna live the life I have.
I don't want other people ruling it for me
Oh just can't you see
I do need other people there for me
But it seems like all they wanna do
Is rule it for me
I just wanna be free.

Weekend
By Thomas

From all the staff
we've had a laugh.
Mixed emotions and tears of sorrow
and not because we're going tomorrow.
We've had to talk through
Some delicate stuff
as most of our lives
have been tough.
Experiences good and bad
People thinking you are mad.
But we cope
By cracking a joke
or having the
occasional smoke.
The people are really understanding
To whatever your age,
woman or man.

So I'd like to say
Now we're on our way.
We've really had a
good few days.

Untitled (1)
By Thomas

Is it you or is it me?
Who wants life to be
Perfect?
Nobody calling you thick.
Treated with respect.
We are an individual
With so much time to kill.
Think about others.
Love one another
as in God's eyes
you're my
sisters and brothers.

Untitled (2)
By Thomas

Please don't ask me why
i laugh and i cry
in my heart full of sorrow
what about tomorrow
what will it bring
will everything be alright
through the day through the night
don't ask me if i feel alright
the answer would be no
as I let my feelings show
when I'm feeling low.

Life
By Thomas

There's times in your life
Where you wanna be free
I've tried it and it's good for me
Learn to be independent once in a while
Learn to be happy
Go on and smile
You only live once they say
So enjoy life day by day.

Company
By Thomas

What is right, What is wrong
Go to the lyrics of that song
I listen to it when I am down
When it's peaceful and I settle down
In front of the fire
I don't need drugs
To get me higher
I just need company
That's all I want
Friendship if anybody's interested
In talking to me.

Crying
By Alex

It can come when you least expect
It can be such a beast
But it's very hard to stop
Especially when it happens a lot.

It can come when you're
Sad, angry or up in your room
It can come in the shower,
When it's hot or when its cold
Even when you're really old.

Untitled (1)
By Alex

Another night, another dream,
Just a scream I did expect.

It seems so real,
Like a vision of death,
That seems to be true,
Caused by hate – hate
Of me.

Hate too bad to be caused
By alcohol or by drugs.

There can only be one
Explanation for their
Actions,
And that explanation
Is me.

Untitled (2)
By Alex

You're bad
That's what you told me
You'll always be sad
That's what you told me
You wont be good till you give us a kiss
That's what you told me
You wont be happier till you give us a shag
That's what you told me

You made me bad
I wont always be sad
You took the piss
You're a fucking drag!!!

You were wrong!!!

Untitled (3)
By Alex

Pools of sadness beneath happy eyes,
The fear of people hearing cries,
Had to tell so many lies.
Had to say so many byes.

Can a new pain, Take away an old pain?
Can a knife, take a life?

Self hatred and punishment,
Am I straight or am I bent?
They don't see the dirt inside
Wish there was a life guide.

Can I ask and forget the past?
Can I sleep and not need to weep?
Can I kill the bloody creeps?

Untitled (4)
By Alex

There's something I'd like to ask my dad – if it
happened to him as a lad – maybe that's what made
him mad.

I gotta know, I gotta know why he liked me feeling so low.

Why cant I put it aside
Even for a day
A ray of light – its ahead
Even though I'm not able to see.

My eyes like water falls
I still remember all my calls
Sorry, please don't, sorry.

I cry, I try but I cant buy their care.

Paula said to my mother
Kill the bitch – wait where's the fun in that
A kick, a punch, know lunch, thrown off a wall
That might do the trick

Untitled (5)
By Alex

Every time that I sleep,
I hear them, I feel them,
Every step forward
Feels like a step back.

Demanding silence,
Trying to understand,
Where do I belong,
Feeling so unsafe,
I wish I had a cave,
A place to go and hide.

Scared and all alone
Where did I go wrong?
Don't understand the meaning of hurt
Got right and wrong the opposite way round
Not allowed to stay.

Untitled (6)
By Alex

I'm really bad, so I feel really sad
I'm looking for a reason
It hasn't been a good season.

Why me, why me, why me
I'm not guilty of a crime
All I did was need
A little food, a little love.

What's the point in life?
I don't see any point
How much can I bear
When I know they didn't care.

Untitled (7)
By Alex

It was so long ago, but it's all coming back
I had pushed it to the back of my mind
So why have I had to find it now.

When they touched me like they did
When they hit me, when they threatened me
Its all coming hour by hour, day by day
Its all coming back.

It was a long time ago, yet I cant stop dreaming
Waking up screaming, it comes in my sleep
Night after night, it comes in my room when I'm all alone
It comes in school through the look in those around
It's all coming back, back to me.

When it comes I cant move
When it comes I cant talk
When it comes I cant be strong
Coz I know its all my fault

Untitled (8)
By Alex

I need to know why,
Why can't I stop shaking
Why can't I stop hiding
Why can't I stop going wrong?

I need to know why,
Nine years of my life I'm told one thing,
And 6 years another

I need to know why,
I'm so confused
I can't keep up with my thoughts
I'm not able to understand
What I done so wrong,

Trying to stop crying
Trying to stop hiding
Trying to stop shaking
Trying to stop getting hurt
Takes far too long. Too long

I need to know to know how,
How to justice
How I know I will escape
The fears of rape
How

Untitled (9)
By Alex

Been up most the night crying
There are things to do
Another scar to try and hide
Another reason I must find.

1 step further to breaking
I wonder how I'll ever make it through this living
nightmare

It's hard to find relief
Hearing so much of their belief
Give me a moment please
I'm gonna fall apart
Gotta go get some relief.

Think about it all the time
Tell me this isn't true
Stop me thinking it
People say I'm free
So why am I panicking, why do I still feel sad
Have nightmares every night and flashbacks
Every day.

Move, move, move away from me
Touch hurts, boys suck
I need some luck, I'm stuck
Cant move, only shake
I don't want to break.

Why O Why?
By Indie Larma

When will I be able to write a song,
Why is it that things go wrong,
Should I just give it up as a bad job,
Or should I look to the skys' and be thanking God?

So I write poems about emotions that hurt,
I write about people that treat me like dirt,
I write about all the things that are bad,
Why do I always feel so sad?

Chorus.
Why oh why was I born this way,
Why do I feel Ive got something to say,
Why oh why,
Why oh why,
Why was I born this way.

Can I not write about the sun that is shining,
Why has it got to be about me that is whining,
I try to write about love and happiness,
But all I can come up with is this crap.

So im sat at the computer working this out,
My head, my life, whats it all about,
Why so many questions that plague me now,
Supposed to be getting easier not causing this row.

<u>Chorus.</u>
Why oh why was I born this way,
Why do I feel Ive got something to say,
Why oh why,
Why oh why,
Why was I born to stay.

<u>Chorus.</u>
Why oh why was I born this way,
Why do I feel Ive got something to say,
Why should people listen anyway,
Why oh why oh why.

Camps
By Indie Larma

I'm deeply affected by this it is true,
I can't stop feeling rather blue.

Round and round my emotions go
Where they are going, nobody knows.

Karen is weak, she is prey for others
She's just the type of meat for fathers.

I have witnessed now, what I went through then
I think that's why I'm going round the bend.

I can't get a grip, I can't slow down
I want to cry, I'm going to drown.

I need a cuddle, I want to be held
To be told its alright, I'm trapped in HELL!!!!

Black Void
By Indie Larma

Oh black void
What do you want?
To drag me down
And you shall be crowned

That I am so thick
That I am so bad
A victim of the past
My type has been cast

But the adult shouts no!
She wants to achieve
Praise from her friends
She wants to believe

The struggle is internal
A crashing war rages
Black and white, red and blue
Fills the many pages!

A Different Day
By Indie Larma

It's a different day
And I feel good
I feel positive and happy
And learnered as I think I should

Its not so confusing
Im getting the drift
The big black downer
Has had time to shift

Today has been fun
I've felt on a level
Equal in intellect
To the others

It's scary when the cloud descends
I try desperately to defend
Myself through the fog and mist
I go to pot, cry a lot, feel like shit
Like to beat myself up a bit
Then the fog lifts, through a haze
and the summer rays, shine down
come to crown, and I almost cry
with a sigh of RELIEF!!!!

Venom
By Indie Larma

I have the strength
You have the power
Working your way
In a covert manner

Clever little thing
Like a spider weaving its web
Slowly working your way
Into my head

You worked your poison
Made me bite
Now I decide
Fight or flight?

The venom is fired
The demon goes down
But for how long
Can I keep my crown?

The Key to Love
By Sue

The key to love is knowing.
The willingness to understand
Unspoken words, the gestures
That mean so much by themselves.

The key to love is forgiving.
The ability not to forget mistakes,
Each other's faults,
But to remember and learn from them.

The key to love is conquering.
Facing the good and bad times,
Searching together
For ways to secure your happiness.

The key to love is in everyone,
Take time to learn,
And unlock the barriers
That keep you from sharing a bond.

The key to love is for the taking,
And leads you to a threshold
That demands great care
But the rewards are there to share

For an Infant
By Sue

I am newly born; and yet
Lived for a thousand years
With hopes and fears: oh hear me

I am newly born; but know
Of sins that are in me
For a world to commit.

I am newly born; forgive me
For my thoughts are my soul
And are here to guide me.

I am newly born; help me
To know the parts to play
In death and in living.

I am newly born; provide for me
A place in which to trust
Where ghosts and ghouls shall wither

I am newly born; protect me
From walls that threaten
And lies which lure.

I am newly born; encourage me
To learn the skills to speak
Of secrets from a saddened heart.

I am newly born; entrust me
With my destiny.

Cryin'
By Sue

Baby stop your cryin'
Cos it hurts down deep
Inside of me.
The pain is just the sorrow
Of life just filled with torment
When I look into a mirror
All I see is ugly misery.
Or the face of my redeemer
A demon staring back at me.
When I grew into a woman
I was scared of what
You might become.
But instead you were the stronger one
And me, well just the lonely scum.
In the dark, black windy night time
I lie and cry alone
And wonder why I came here
And see just what I have become.
Spoke little from inside of me
And yet I was so happy
In my world of sheer despondency
A woman or a weapon.
My Daddy was a sad man
And yet he loved me endlessly
His final breath was drawn alone
Why could I not then be with him.

Depressive State
By Vera

Solitude confinement in a space of time,
Lonely isolated in thoughts and rhyme.
The window to the world so bleak and bare,
Uncaring as people strive to exist unaware.
Life is consumed by the greed of those with power,
Those who destroy the future and wealth devour.
Persecute a child newly born without concern,
And the aged are cursed they will greedily confirm.

Ask for help and they will reject a need,
Watching with pleasure vast poverty plead.
The chosen few will live in prosperous leisure
Wining and dining without effort or endeavour.
I deplore riches and unearned wealth,
Bigots and cheats who earn by stealth.
Rob the poor the sick and the old,
And bedeck themselves with diamonds and gold.

Branded as poor you have no voice,
Still you provided the wealth for which they rejoice.
When you had a job and earned your pay,
You paid to work so the wealthy could stay.
Workers created the wealth of this nation,
Then the rich created high inflation.
Industry is becoming a thing of the past,
How far into the future will the rich last

Home
By Vera

I stood and looked as change took place,
Carefully watching each new face.
Seeing no more the home I knew,
And people I know well only a few.
Some have moved or been laid to rest,
It's hard to know which for them was best.
My sister is much older now,
And lives as age and time allows.
Father's grave is covered with weeds,
Nobody sees to it's paltry needs.

My old home now is dust and rubble,
But as a family it shared our troubles.
It was small and neat and warm,
Sheltering us from all life's harm.
Filled with love and gentle care,
Laughter and joy it too did share.
Now I have a home of my own,
And all these qualities it has shown.
It comforts me when I am alone,
And to me it now is home.

Lost Love
By Vera

An empty chair where he once sat,
Where he would sit and gaily chat.
His face I see in a photograph,
I imagine I can hear him laugh.
Life without him won't be the same,
He won't reply when I call his name.
Happy memories I still recall,
For those I treasure above all.
A certain smile that was just for me,
I close my eyes and again I can see.
The way he closed the garden gate,
It is silent now though I still wait.
And though my love he did spurn,
I still await his return.
The emptiness I now feel within,
Is something that should not have been.

Rebecca
By Vera

Born to love and bring you joy,
Your little girl

A little stranger yours to behold,
Rebecca is worth her weight in gold.
Precious to you both in every way,
Your little beauty is here to stay.
A tiny smile will thrill you so much,
As did at birth that very first touch.
You will help her learn and grow,
Always your love you must give and show.

We are proud to be counted as friends,
And pray this relationship will never end.
Your first born is a joy to behold,
A part of your future in growing old.
Sharing with you all aspects of life,
Until the day she becomes a wife.
Sharing her life with a special boy,
But with you she will share her joy.

A mother is special in every way,
And father too has a role to play.
He gives each moment he can spare,
Showing love and how much he cares.
Our children learn all through life,
Joy and sadness hurt and strife,
How to trust and laughter at play.

Untitled (1)
By Vera

A true friend I have but one,
Sincere honest caring yet so much fun
A friend who listens in times of stress,
Her very precious existence I bless.
Unlike others who call me friend,
But use me to better their own ends.
I respect those who are true and sincere,
And deplore all bigots and always feed on fear.

Many will hold out a hand to take,
To ask for help is a grave mistake.
I tell myself help is near,
But to ask creates a deep felt fear.
I do not want gold or jewels,
But simple things to keep out the cold,
Simple things and needs are out of reach,
I dare not ask the refusal is bleak.

My life has no meaning or cheer,
Each day is misery and so drear.
The past was filled with pain and regret
What I have now is a hopeless concept.
Nothing to do no place in life,
Used and abused and endless strife.
Others come to me with worries and woes,
But my life is to end with no place to go.

Untitled (2)
By Vera

Life is a way of learning the way,
To work and care for others each day.
Wisdom and knowledge make us grow,
For the earth is a stage for the show.
We give to others what lessons we learn,
Teach love and caring then respect we will earn.
Share wealth with those who need a friend,
Caring and sharing must never end.

Each day is a blessing and full of love,
It was sent to us from heaven above.
When pain is with us we must not frown,
Never allow ill health to get you down.
Care for your loved ones and don't dismay,
Though angry words you often will say.
You always hurt the ones you love,
Be it here on earth or in heaven above.

When you speak to a loved one who passed away,
They will hear you by night or day.
When you're alone and utter a sigh,
Being unaware who stands at your side.
A gentle touch or a feeling you know,
You are with loved ones visiting from above.
They care and watch your every move,
And comfort you in sadness believe me it's proved.

Untitled (3)
By Vera

Pain and weariness on long days,
Makes time reach out in many ways.
Peace at last is near and waits,
Departure through a pearly gate.
Sleep so long and yet so deep,
Pictures of loved for whom I did weep.
They wait for me and will ask me in,
No sign of anger and not recalling sin.

Going home is a thing of joy,
Loved ones around me like when I was a boy,

My life is before me a wondrous sight,
Days are long with still dark nights.
As here in my bed I do lie,
Remembering brings forth long deep sighs.
Regrets are many as I relive my life,
Joy and sorrow also sadness and strife.

What awaits me I have yet to learn,
Peace and goodness for which I yearn.
Pain and weariness on long days,
Makes time reach out in so many ways.
Sleep so long and yet so deep,
Loved ones a vigil over me will keep
They wait for me and will ask me in,
And remind me of things that have been.

Untitled (4)
By Vera

Life in this house is a constant pain,
A dull ache with no cure to gain.
Torments and suffering a strange insanity,
Robbed of all decent thoughts mindless yet free.
Disgust is relished and hate enjoyed,
People are never treated with respect but annoyed.
Being spoken to in a lowly way,
A constant thing each disgusting day.

No love exists in this house of shame,
Only lust and lies they are all the same.
Unbearable the crowded room became,
A prison a house without a name.
No warmth is felt from the people within,
But hate flows freely escorted by sin.
Laughter is never in fun or play,
But is heard in a harsh sarcastic way.

When life in this house is no more,
It won't be missed and its vagrant laws.
Hard times to suffer in silent pain,
Nothing lost but then nothing gained.
So when this is an empty shell,
No abode no place which in we dwell.

Remember the hurt sorrow and strife,
Then say to hell with a miserable life.

Untitled
By Denise

As I walk down a lonely street
I think people are there to get me
I look all around and then I panic
Rushing round to get back home.

Why do I panic and run away?
Only people I tell will ever know
It's because of the hurt
That I've always suffered.

And because of all that is why I am
Panicking, shaking, running away
And some day soon I'll be OK
Being there not running away.
For I haven't done anything wrong
No nothing wrong at all.

CHAPTER 11

Exercises for Adult Victims

When working with those who have suffered abuse in order to enhance healing, an objective will be to help the person talk about the abuse they have experienced. Being able to sit and talk openly is good, but the purpose of this book as stated in the introduction is to demonstrate how people can also be encouraged to express themselves through writing. Some people may find it very difficult (or even impossible) just to sit down and write. Undertaking exercises may be one method that can be employed to encourage expression through writing and drawing. This chapter will present exercises which have been tried and tested in the Beyond Existing groups. People who may engage in exercises will be referred to as participants.

Why do exercises?

The word 'exercise' might be off-putting to some people; perhaps because it sounds like a task that had to be undertaken at school, and this could bring back bad memories. Exercises might be associated with tests. In group work an exercise should be something that participants can enjoy and learn from; it should not be something that is feared.

Objectives in using exercises should be for participants to:

- think
- reflect

- encourage verbalisation
- express feelings
- identify areas to work on
- set targets and time limits for the future.

Handout 11.1, p.227

Many victims find it difficult to talk about the abuse they have experienced; it can be very hard and painful to revisit what was done to them. In order to heal, a victim must relive what was done to them and express how they felt at the time and now at the time of healing. Over time victims will have developed their own coping strategies, however, the task for group leaders is to help victims develop strategies to heal. The following exercises are designed to help victims express their feelings in a creative way. Group leaders will learn what areas need more work as the needs of victims will differ. Work will involve:

- developing a positive image of oneself/build self-esteem
- gaining an understanding into why abuse happens
- dispelling any feelings of self-blame
- setting objectives
- developing coping strategies for the future.

Ground rules

Whenever group work is being undertaken clear ground rules should be set at the beginning (see Chapters 7, 8 and 9). In Beyond Existing it was made clear that no one would be forced to do anything they did not want to do. People need to feel safe before participating in exercises; that is, trust has to be developed between participants themselves and with the leaders. The following ground rules were agreed by one of the Beyond Existing groups as the group was set up.

Ground rules

At the first meeting of the group, the following ground rules were agreed by members:

1. This group is run for the benefit of its members.

2. No one has to speak or participate unless they want to do so.

3. Everyone can have his/her say.

4. Only one person will speak at any one time.

5. Everyone will respect each other, even if we have different opinions.

6. No one will be judgemental.

7. No one will criticise anybody else.

8. No one will be rejected or made to feel rejected.

9. Everything that is said in the group is confidential. Exceptions:

    (a) If we thought you were going to harm yourself or others.
    (b) If we learnt a child was currently being abused we have a duty to report under the Children Act 1989.

10. There will be breaks and refreshments.

Although these ground rules were developed for the running of the group generally, they were very helpful in creating a safe environment for participants to engage in exercises which encouraged them to speak openly about their feelings. The leaders often reread the ground rules to the group before an exercise was undertaken. It is very important that participants are not hindered by the fear that someone will criticise or laugh at them, which is what their abuser may have done in the past.

It is important that leaders explain exactly what is going to happen, to allay any fears and to state that no one will be forced to do anything they do not want to do. Some participants may be very apprehensive initially. Denise remembers clearly how she felt when the leaders said they would like the group to participate in a group exercise: 'I thought, "You're not getting me to do that crap".'

The first exercise Denise participated in involved the leader writing responses from the group on a flipchart (Exercise 11.2 below). After a very short while, Denise volunteered to do the writing and thereafter often was proactive in writing on behalf of the group.

Particular difficulties

It would be hoped that by the time the idea of doing exercises was introduced the leaders would have acquired some basic information about the participants. Before attending most groups, participants would have been screened in some way. It is important that leaders are aware of any particular problems a participant might have and not to make assumptions. For example, a common difficulty is that many older people cannot read or write. In this day and age younger workers may assume that everyone has had an education; many older people have not and may have left school at a very early age. Such people may be very good at covering up the fact that they cannot read and write. In a group it could be very embarrassing for someone to admit they have literacy problems. Once a person feels safe in a group, they may be able to talk freely about their difficulties and with support can engage in the exercises. In Beyond Existing groups where participants could not read or write, a leader would work with the individual; that is, the participants would tell the leader what they wanted written down. There were occasions when agreement was reached with other participants that the participant's social worker would come into the group meeting and help the participant.

Examples of problems encountered in Beyond Existing are:

- literacy
- poor eye sight
- hearing problems
- learning disabilities affecting communication skills
- physical disabilities affecting mobility
- mental capacity issues.

Therefore, before suggesting that an exercise be undertaken, leaders should consider whether participants can:

- see
- hear
- read
- write
- understand
- communicate their difficulties
- move around.

 Handout 11.2, p.228

Facilities and equipment

Leaders will have considered whether the venue is suitable for the needs of the group. When considering using exercises as a method of working, it will be important to consider whether:

- The room is big enough: that is, is there enough space for participants to spread out or if necessary to work alone and privately with a leader?
- The right equipment is available.

Equipment needed may include:

- flipchart stand
- flipchart paper
- flipchart pens
- journals
- notebooks
- paper
- pens
- Sellotape
- Blu-Tack

 Handout 11.3, p.229

Working with participants

In the following pages 12 exercises will be presented which can be used by workers in a group setting; some of them can also be undertaken as individual work. Explanations will be given using the following headings:

- Objective
- Equipment
- Time
- Task
- Discussion
- Note for leaders.

An assumption is made that no more than eight people will participate in an exercise. If a group is larger or smaller than this number, then the leaders should allow more or less time than stated. The time suggested does *not* include introduction/explanation by the leaders.

The text will refer to 'leaders' in the plural, as most groups are likely to be facilitated by two leaders rather than one.

Typing up work

Some work produced in exercises may need to be typed up afterwards and given to the participants, so that it becomes part of a record of what has been achieved and/or it can be referred back to when reassessing progress. Leaders need to ensure that they have the time and facilities to do this. Some examples of work produced by members of Beyond Existing will be given below as exercises are described.

FUTURE WORK

Objective

It is important in any group that is working with adults who have been abused that there should be some focus on the future, that is, what do participants want to achieve within set time limits? If a participant is feeling particularly low, it can be hard to think positively about the future. This exercise will facilitate participants to share their hopes and fears for the future. It can also help to lay the foundations for future work to be undertaken in the group.

Equipment

Notebook and pen

Time

One hour

Task

1. Participants think about the future in general and what they hope to achieve.

2. The leader then asks participants to think about particular time periods, for example (i) 1 month, 6 months, 12 months; (ii) 6 months, 1 year, 5 years.

3. Participants write down their objectives for the set time periods.

Discussion

Participants share their objectives with the group. Each participant is given adequate time to talk about their hopes and fears for the future.

Notes for leaders

1. Leaders need to decide what they hope to achieve from this exercise. It can be a very good exercise to use when a group is just starting in order to set some targets. Sometimes it can be better to set small timescales because participants may find it easier to focus on the immediate future rather than the far-distant future. This is especially true for participants who are struggling to get through each day.

2. As stated above some people can find it hard to focus or plan for the future. Therefore, participants may need individual help from leaders when undertaking this exercise.

3. If the group is still running when the set timescales have been reached, it is vital for the leaders to put time aside in a meeting to revisit this exercise. Discussion should focus on what participants have achieved, but consideration should also be given to why some objectives have not been managed. This should be done sensitively so that it is not seen as a negative experience. It is then possible to set realistic objectives for the future.

MEANING OF WORDS

Objective
Many different words are used to describe a person who has been abused. It can be enlightening for participants to explain what particular words mean to them.

Equipment
Flipchart stand, paper and pens

Time
30 minutes

Task
A word is written by a leader on the flipchart paper. Working as a large group, participants are asked to say what the word means to them.

Discussion
Discussion usually develops naturally as this exercise progresses. Additional time can be set aside to discuss what has evolved on the flipchart sheets.

Notes for leaders
1. Key words which can be used for this exercise:
    Victim
    Survivor
    Abuse
    Abuser

2. Victims of abuse can feel stigmatised and discriminated against. Their experiences of how

WORK FROM BEYOND EXISTING (EXERCISE 11.2)

What the word 'victim' means to you

- Abuse – ongoing
- Lose all self-esteem
- Suffering – still
- Pain in head
- Physical pain
- Emotional pain
- Spiritual suffering
- Screwing your mind
- Happy go lucky
- Worthless
- Dirty
- Vulnerable
- Migraine
- Nerves in teeth
- Sad
- Ugly
- Sense of humour
- Sensitivity
- Empathy

What the word 'survivor' means to you

- I don't know I will survive this
- Be happy again
- What's that?
- Still here
- Resilient
- Strength
- Talk
- Honest
- Open
- Trusting
- See things for what they really are
- Protective
- Goods

WHAT WE HAVE IN COMMON

Objective
Very often when working with groups it becomes evident that many participants have a great deal in common. Victims often say at some point that in the past they have felt that abuse had *only* happened to them, and that their fear would be that no one would believe them if they talked about their experiences. This is particularly true for older people who earlier in life were not encouraged to talk about intimate experiences and feelings. The main objective of this exercise is to show that participants in a group probably have a lot in common and this will promote feelings of safety while working in the group.

Equipment
Flipchart stand, paper, pens

Time
45 minutes

Task
The leader asks the group to say what they think they have in common.

Discussion
The leader will facilitate the discussion and encourage commonalities regarding abusive experiences.

Notes for leaders
This exercise needs to be undertaken when participants in a group have known each other for some time.

WORK FROM BEYOND EXISTING (EXERCISE 11.3)

Things group members have in common

1. Child abuse:
   - mental
   - physical
   - sexual

   Happened between ages of 5 and 23

2. Domestic violence:
   - alcohol-related
   - harassment

3. Adult abuse:
   - mental
   - physical
   - financial

4. A chance meeting
5. Attending hospital
6. Seeing a psychiatrist
7. Puts you off men
8. Mothers – needing to confront them
9. Loss of possessions
10. No trust
11. Walked away from abuse
12. Loss of children (death, fostered, no contact)
13. Bereavement
14. Loss of confidence
15. Loss of people/loved ones
16. Loss of memories

When talking about the healing process and how survivors make progress then take some steps backwards, Pat said:

> 'You've got to step back to look at life before you can go forward.'

DEALING WITH FEAR

Objective

All victims will have experienced feelings of fear while being abused. These feelings may be rekindled when memories are triggered – especially when working through the healing process. This exercise will demonstrate the various coping strategies developed by victims, and how by sharing these, victims can develop further coping strategies for the future.

Equipment

Notebook and pen

Time

45 minutes

Task

Participants write down three occasions when they have experienced fear and what they did to cope with the situation.

Discussion

Each participant shares their experiences.

Notes for leaders

Some participants may become very distressed when undertaking this exercise and may need to take time out from the group and receive additional support from a leader.

BEING SAFE

Objective
Some participants may still be living in an abusive situation when attending a group. It can be useful to have a session on 'keeping safe'. Other participants may be able to offer help and support about how they kept themselves safe. It is helpful in general to get participants to think what makes them feel safe now.

Equipment
Notebook and pen

Time
45 minutes

Task
Participants list:

1. Times in their lives when they have felt unsafe

2. What would have made them feel safe

3. What makes them feel safe now

Discussion

1. Participants share their writings.

2. The leader puts to the group the question: 'What makes a person feel safe?'

Notes for leaders
The leader needs to focus the group on both practical and emotional matters regarding safety.

AN OBJECT

Objective
To identify the way in which different things can help a person survive a difficult situation.

Equipment
None

Time
10 minutes for each participant

Task
Participants are asked to bring to the next session an object which was important or special to them because it helped them at a difficult time or gave them strength in a certain situation.

Discussion
Each participant explains the significance of the object.

Notes for leaders
There have been occasions when participants have continued to bring objects when they felt the need. It can be helpful to say that it is okay to do this after the exercise has been completed.

WORK FROM BEYOND EXISTING (EXERCISE 11.6)

Some objects which have been brought for this exercise include:

- photograph

- designs/plans produced when working as a draughtswoman

- child's plastic bracelet

- earrings

- poems

- doll.

HAPPY AND SAD TIMES

Objective
To help participants realise that they have had both good and bad experiences which have led them through a wide range of emotions. When working with issues associated with abuse, participants sometimes think they are only allowed to talk about their negative experiences. But some victims will have had positive experiences and have good memories which they are uncertain whether they should express. A victim can also have some good feelings about the abuser and should not be afraid to express these.

Equipment
Notebook and pen

Time
45 minutes

Task
Participants list:

1. Three times when they have been sad

2. Three times when they have been happy

Discussion
Participants talk about the sad times followed by the happy times, so that the discussion can finish on a positive note.

Notes for leaders
1. This exercise can be used as a way of getting victims to talk about how the abuse/abuser has made them feel.

2. It is important to bring out the positive feelings within the group.

STRENGTHS AND WEAKNESSES

Objective
To help participants to recognise their inner strengths, but also to identify weaknesses which they need to work on.

Equipment
Participants work in their notebooks.
The leader will use flipchart stand, paper and pens.

Time
One hour

Task
Participants list their own:

1. Strengths

2. Weaknesses

Discussion

1. One by one each participant shares their list.

2. Other group members are asked to share their views about the strengths of that person.

3. One leader uses the flipchart sheet to list strengths and weaknesses in two columns.

4. After full discussion, participants are asked to set objectives for themselves: that is, what other strengths they want to strive for and which weaknesses they want to work on.

Notes for leaders

1. Very often other participants will see strengths in a person which they themselves do not see. This can be a good way of promoting positive self-esteem.

2. The leaders should discourage any negative comments about any participant. It can be useful to set a special ground rule (or revisit original ground rules if appropriate) so that no one feels threatened or under attack.

3. It can be a positive help to get the list that has been compiled on the flipchart paper typed up for participants to keep. It will show and reinforce the strengths within the group.

WORK FROM BEYOND EXISTING (EXERCISE 11.8)

Strengths

- Artistic
- Determined
- Doing what I want to do
- Enjoy it
- Being retired
- Compassion
- Caring
- Being able to share with others
- Happy
- Intelligent
- Nice to get on with
- Honest
- Confronting the pain
- Attractive
- Role model
- Mother figure
- Defend children
- Sweet

LIKES, DISLIKES AND CHANGE

Objective

Many victims of abuse have low self-esteem. This is often due to the fact that the abuser has told them they are useless, worthless etc. A crucial part of the healing process is to help victims understand that often their perception of themselves is unduly negative and unjustly so. The objective of this exercise is to promote self-worth.

Equipment

Notebook and pen
Flipchart stand, paper, pens

Time

One hour

Task

Participants are asked to:

1. Put a line down the middle of a page in the notebook.

2. Write at the top of one column 'What I like about myself...'

3. Write at the top of the other column 'What I dislike about myself...'

4. Participants are given ten minutes to write in the columns.

Discussion

1. Each participant shares their lists.

2. The leader uses the flipchart sheet to list likes and dislikes in two columns.

3. Other participants are asked what they like about that particular person and these comments are added to the 'Likes' column.

4. The leaders should discourage any negative comments about any participant. It can be useful to set a special ground rule (or revisit original ground rules if appropriate) so that no one feels threatened or under attack.

5. After a full discussion participants work in their notebooks again. They list what they would like to change about themselves.

6. Group discussion then focuses on how these changes can take place.

7. The changes and methods to be used are then written as objectives, with realistic timescales set for review at future meetings.

Notes for leaders

It may be necessary to allow some extra time to discuss how participants feel about 'change' in general. Although a victim may feel ready to move on in their life, the thought of instigating changes may feel very threatening or unsafe, because of the coping strategies they already have developed and have in place.

AMBITIONS AND FULFILMENT

Objective
It is important to acknowledge that the meaning of happiness will be interpreted differently by each individual because everyone is unique. Going through the healing process must involve encouraging victims to express how they could be fulfilled and helping them to realise their ambitions. This exercise will encourage participants to focus on the future.

Equipment
Notebook and pen

Time
45 minutes

Task
Participants list what would need to happen to make them happy in the future, that is, events, surprises, relationships, achievements.

Discussion
1. Each participant shares his or her hopes and fears regarding achieving happiness.

2. Participants make suggestions how happiness can be achieved.

3. Participants set themselves targets to achieve happiness.

Notes for leaders
Although in discussion there may be a great deal of wistful fun, like waving a magic wand, winning the lottery, marrying a dream person and so on, it is important for leaders to ensure that the final targets are realistic.

A SOAP OPERA

Objective
This exercise is designed to help participants undertake a life review.

Equipment
Journal and pen

Time
This exercise should be undertaken over a number of sessions. Work will be done by participants in between meetings.

Task
1. Participants are told that they have been commissioned to write a soap opera which has six episodes.

2. Participants reflect on their life and divide it up into six important episodes. Each episode is given a title.

3. Over six sessions participants will write about each episode in their life.

Discussion
Participants will read from their journal at future sessions.

Notes for leaders
Leaders need to be aware that a variety of emotions can be presented when participants share their work and time can be taken up dealing with these. Therefore, leaders need to allow enough time for unexpected events in this exercise, so that participants are not rushed at the end of the session.

THE SNAKE

Objective

In order to move on in their lives victims have to deal with the past. This exercise can be used as a way of finding out more about a person and what past events need to be dealt with in order to heal. The objective of the exercise is to get a participant to do a life review through drawing and writing and to identify events in life which need to be worked on.

Equipment

Flipchart paper and pens

Time

One hour

Task

1. Each participant is given a flipchart sheet and a variety of coloured pens.

2. Participants think about the major events (both good and bad) that have occurred in their life.

3. Participants are asked to draw a snake with bends in its body. Each bend signifies a major event in life. Each bend is dated.

Discussion

1. Each participant presents their snake to the rest of the group by summarising the key events and how they feel about those events now.

2. Events are identified for future work.

Notes for leaders

1. This is a very useful exercise to find out more about people and what has happened to them in the past.

2. This exercise can be used to plan future individual or group work.

3. This can, however, be a very painful exercise for some participants as it may trigger memories and feelings that are difficult to cope with. Leaders should very sensitively ensure that participants are not forced or do not feel obliged to talk publicly about such painful memories. Some participants may be in two minds whether to speak. It may therefore be necessary for some individual work to be done in a private area.

 # WORK FROM BEYOND
EXISTING (EXERCISE 11.12)

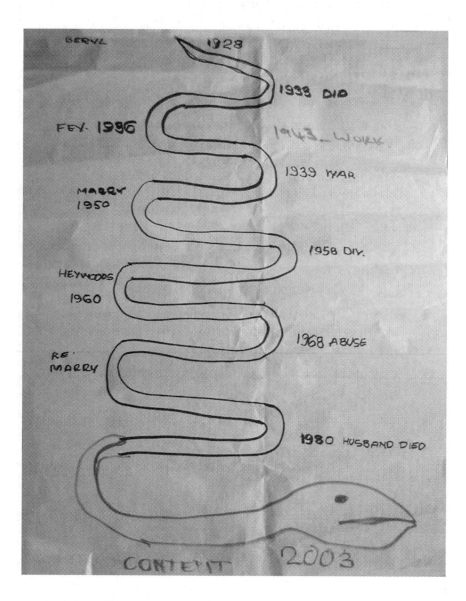

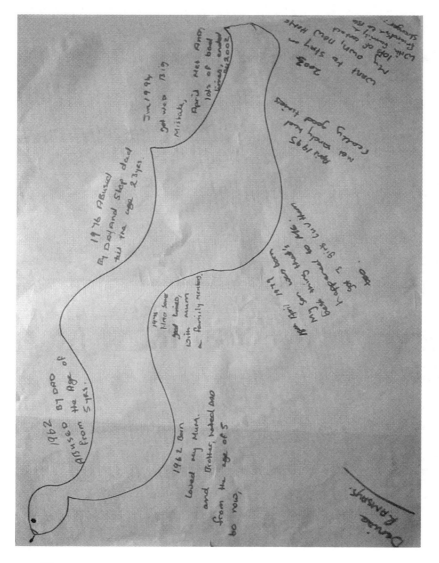

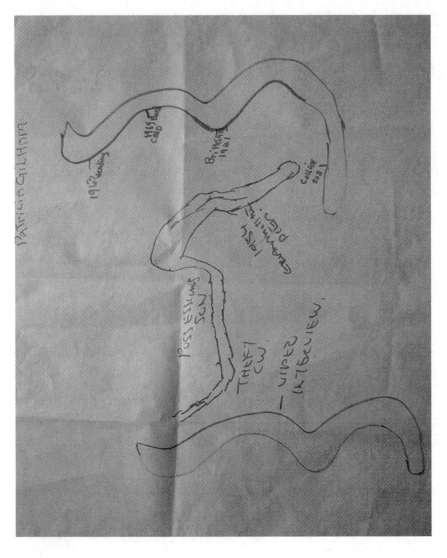

226

OBJECTIVES IN UNDERTAKING EXERCISES

Through engaging in exercises, participants will be encouraged to:

- Think

- Reflect

- Encourage verbalisation

- Express feelings

- Identify areas to work on

- Set targets and time limits for the future

CONSIDERATIONS FOR LEADERS USING EXERCISES

Can participants:

- See?

- Hear?

- Read?

- Write?

- Understand?

- Communicate their difficulties?

- Move around?

EQUIPMENT NEEDED FOR EXERCISES

- Flipchart stand

- Flipchart paper

- Flipchart pens

- Journals

- Notebooks

- Paper

- Pens

- Sellotape

- Blu-Tack

References

Arnold, L. and Babiker, G. (1998) 'Counselling people who self-injure.' In Z. Bear (ed) *Good Practice in Counselling People Who Have Been Abused*. London: Jessica Kingsley Publishers.

Birren, J.E. and Birren, B.A. (1996) 'Autobiography: Exploring the self and encouraging development.' In J. Birren, G. Kenyon, J.E. Ruth, J. Schroots and T. Svensson (eds) *Aging and Biography*. New York: Springer.

Bolton, G. (1999) *The Therapeutic Potential of Creative Writing*. London: Jessica Kingsley Publishers.

Bornat, J. (ed.) (1994) *Reminiscence Reviewed: Perspectives, Evaluations and Achievements*. Buckingham: Open University Press.

Coulshed, V. (1991) *Social Work Practice*. Birmingham: BASW/Macmillan.

Department of Health (2000a) *No Secrets: Guidance on Developing and Implementing Multi-agency Policies and Procedures to Protect Vulnerable Adults from Abuse*. London: HMSO.

Department of Health (2000b) *No Secrets: Guidance on Developing and Implementing Multi-agency Policies and Procedures to Protect Vulnerable Adults from Abuse*. Health Service/Local Authority Circular HSC 2000/007. London: NHS Executive.

Department of Health, Department of Education and Employment, Home Office (2000) *Framework for the Assessment of Children in Need and their Families*. London: The Stationery Office.

Department of Health, Home Office, Department of Education and Employment (1999) *Working Together to Safeguard Children: A Guide to Inter-agency Working to Safeguard and Promote the Welfare of Children*. London: The Stationery Office.

Etherington, K. (2000) *Narrative Approaches to Working with Adult Male Survivors of Child Sexual Abuse*. London: Jessica Kingsley Publishers.

Gibson, F. (1998) *Reminiscence and Recall: A Guide to Good Practice* (Second edition). London: Age Concern.

Hunt, C. and Sampson, F. (eds) (1998) *The Self on the Page: Theory and Practice of Creative Writing in Personal Development*. London: Jessica Kingsley Publishers.

Keith-Lucas, A. (1972) *Giving and Taking Help*. Carolina: University of North Carolina Press.

Linde, C. (1993) *Life Stories: The Creation of Coherence*. Oxford: Oxford University Press.

Lord Chancellor's Department (1997) *Who Decides? Making Decisions on Behalf of Mentally Incapacitated Adults*. London: The Stationery Office.

Oxford Compact English Dictionary (Second edition) (2000). Oxford: Oxford University Press.

Payne, M. (2002) 'Social work theories and reflective practice.' In R. Adams, L. Dominelli and M. Payne (eds) *Social Work: Themes, Issues and Critical Debates* (Second edition). London: Palgrave.

Pennebaker, J.W. (1988) 'Confiding traumatic experiences and health.' In S. Fisher and J. Reason (eds) *Handbook of Life Stress, Cognition and Health*. Chichester: Wiley.

Pennebaker, J.W. (1993) 'Putting stress into words: health, linguistic and therapeutic implications.' *Behaviour Research and Therapy 31*, 539–548.

Philips, D., Linington, L. and Penman, D. (1999) *Writing Well: Creative Writing and Mental Health*. London: Jessica Kingsley Publishers.

Pritchard, J. (2000) *The Needs of Older Women: Services for Victims of Elder Abuse and Other Abuse*. Bristol: The Policy Press.

Pritchard, J. (2001) *Male Victims of Elder Abuse: Their Experiences and Needs*. London: Jessica Kingsley Publishers.

Pritchard, J. (2003) *Support Groups for Older People Who Have Been Abused: Beyond Existing*. London: Jessica Kingsley Publishers.

The Reach Out Project: 2000 (2000). Barnardos, North-East Region.

Reid, W.J. and Shyne, A.W. (1969) *Brief and Extended Casework*. New York: Columbia University Press.

Rhodes, M. (1986) *Ethical Dilemmas in Social Work Practice*. London: Routledge and Kegan Paul.

Sainsbury, E., Nixon, S. and Phillips, D. (1982) *Social Work in Focus*. London: Routledge and Kegan Paul.

Williams, R. (2002) *Resurrection*. London: Darton, Longman and Todd.

Subject Index

References to information in the exercises are given exercise numbers as well as page numbers

Author Index